D1534896

Fire in the Hole

A Mortarman in Vietnam

James Michael Orange

Writers Club Press
San Jose New York Lincoln Shanghai

Fire in the Hole
A Mortarman in Vietnam

Writers Club Press
an imprint of iUniverse.com, Inc.

For information address:
iUniverse.com, Inc.
5220 S 16th, Ste. 200
Lincoln, NE 68512
www.iuniverse.com

ISBN: 0-595-16003-4

Printed in the United States of America

Fire in the Hole

Orange has written a powerful book....He has crafted a morally sensitive story that begs for discussion and demands that we remember those whom we sent to fight the Vietnam War-a war that continues to define the next generation. It is our public responsibility to those who fought the Vietnam War to tell their story to the next generation. It is our responsibility to the children of our veterans to tell the story. Orange has done that and more....

—Paul Wellstone, United States Senator

Fire in the Hole is a brutally candid Vietnam memoir written with intense poetic description and a delicate sensitivity, that describes the effects of combat on a human soul. Read it—you won't be able to put it down.

—Mary O'Brien Tyrrell; former Lieutenant, Head Nurse, Air Evac. Unit, U.S. Navy Hospital, Guam, M.I. (1967-1968); current owner, Memoirs, Inc.

I was delighted, sobered, and, frankly, dazzled by the book. It is a compelling and revealing memoir. The almost lyrical writing conveys a soul-wrenching, perhaps even a soul-destroying experience. The introspection comes across as genuine, not preachy, or maudlin. The detailed descriptions force the reader to enter Orange's Vietnam world, to understand the context for his thoughts and actions. Four stars.

—David Morris, Ph.D., Vice President, Institute for Local Self Reliance,
author of five books including *We Must Make Haste Slowly: The Process of Revolution in Chile* (1973)

Orange has written a down-on-the-ground, soldier's book on the Vietnam experience. He paints no picture of himself as hero, but gives us something of the ordinary character of that war while stunning the reader with the pain and realism of 'being there.' I read the book in one sitting.

—Tex Sample, Ph.D., Coordinator, Network for the Study of U.S. Lifestyles, author of six books including *U.S. Lifestyles and Mainline Churches* (1990)

The tale is tragic, terse, and by no means pretty. Orange takes us with him on operations; the dirty, wearisome routine of patrols and perimeters, where there is never a moment of real safety; and along the way we learn how Marines fight, how they kill, and how some of them die. There is cruelty, murder, fear, and there is, in the midst of it all, a single human being, a young American fresh from the college campus, who tries to survive physically and mentally. *Fire in the Hole* is a good read for anyone, veterans and non-veterans, with an interest in the War as seen through the eyes of a Marine grunt.

—John Young, former career Army infantry NCO with thirty months of combat service in Vietnam, university guest lecturer on the Vietnam War.

This is one of those straightforward testimonials that needs to be absorbed. As both a preacher and a Vietnam veteran, I think our souls—both individual and collective—can't be healed until "the rest of the story" is understood as an integral part of our history. Orange tells the story without guile or the need to impress. Read the story. Let it get inside of you. You'll change.

—Davidson Loehr, Ph.D., Minister, First Unitarian Universalist Church of Austin

Orange not only has a great story to tell, he tells it in a way that is interesting and exciting. I couldn't put it down. He drew me in and took me back to my own Vietnam War memories. Orange's tale of surviving the tragedies and horror of war helped his healing. It will help the rest of us as well.

—Barry W. Riesch, President Chapter 27 Minnesota Veterans for Peace, Inc.

The [Vietnam War] continues to hurt both Americans and Vietnamese. If we are attentive enough, we can still learn from the war....Veterans have experience that makes them the light at the tip of the candle; illuminating the roots of war and the way to peace.

—Thich Nhat Hahn, *Peace Is Every Step*

Cynthia: My best friend, my wife and lover, mother to our daughter, wise counselor, and writing teacher. You enrich my life.

Jessica: There were early years when I loved having so much to teach and share with you. Now I love having so much to learn from you.

Veterans of war: I found absolution in the writing. I hope my writing can help others.

Contents

Foreword

I've just finished reading the final draft of Michael's book. "This is a love letter to life," I thought as I closed the last page, hugging his words, his book, tight to my chest. Like most love letters, it is filled with pathos and promises, innocence and pain, and honesty that both warms and terrifies me. Michael's stories are a gift to the world; Michael is an extraordinary gift to me and to Jessica.

Michael and I first met 32 years ago this summer. Our faces were smooth with youthful anticipation, our lives fairly uncomplicated. Tabula rasa. No war, no divorce, no death or loss yet recorded on our predominantly blank slates. Michael went off to march in the war and I marched against it, but our friendship remained unshakable. From the outset we were tethered by some indefinable but pure chord that transcended politics and endured all our individual changes and challenges.

When I married Michael in 1974, I soon discovered I had also married Vietnam. In the long nights of our early marriage, the ghosts of that war often slept between us, preventing caresses. He told no one he met that he was a Vietnam veteran and he wouldn't talk about the war to his family or friends. A couple of months into our marriage, he asked me if the two of us could have a "Vietnam night." After we had tucked Jessica into bed, he spread out his pictures on the desk in the little trailer home we rented in Kent, Ohio.

I listened to his stories deep into that night and began to ache from the weight of that terrible war. My eyes stung from the smoke of burning villages. My body rocked back and forth with the peasants as they hugged themselves tight in their grief. I still remember the name of the little cat—Titi Lau—that was eaten by the rats. I walked in jungle heat with him, saw little boys get blown apart after they exploded a home-made bomb, smelled the pieces of burning flesh as they floated down around me.

Even as a little girl, our daughter knew to be careful not to startle her dad or wake him suddenly. He used to dream about Vietnam a lot—almost every night—when we were first married. I'd lay close, matching my breathing to his own, waiting until his breaths seemed smooth, his sleep restful.

We have a great partnership. Michael's "it's a good day, no one is shooting at me" attitude has rubbed off, and I am blessed to be sharing my life with him. He no longer drops to his belly, hands protecting his neck, body stretched close to the ground, when he hears a car backfire. And he has learned about the danger of silence.

In 1984, Michael worked up the courage to begin speaking to students about his experiences in Vietnam. Each time I hear him do this my heart cracks a little more, but I am grateful that his is healing.

Michael began writing about Vietnam in 1996. As his stories moved from catharsis to craft, he says he moved further from the raw emotion. He showed me the stories and asked me to edit them, "to make them better." I'd respond as a writing teacher and offer concrete advice about "showing and not telling," about the importance of detail and description. But as a wife, a lover, and a best friend, my insides churned as I was again taken to the sights, smells, tastes, sounds, and feelings of Vietnam. I wanted so desperately to "make it better," to kiss his wounds and erase his pain.

My love for my husband—this gentle man, this remarkable father, this talented writer, this patient friend—is fierce. Like so many others who are intimately connected with veterans of war and survivors of battle, I am able to love the warrior and still hate the war. But the war still haunts us every day.

—Cynthia L. Orange, 2000

Preface

I was twenty years old when I went to Vietnam. I am over fifty now. I am a middle-aged man telling stories. These are my truths.

I have recorded here the essence of each story as it happened. I do not have a photographic memory. Most of the time I did not know where I was, where I was going, or why. Nonetheless, each story is burned into my brain, like shrapnel in the marrow of my life all these years later. I have tried to erase some of these memories, but find I cannot. The smells are still pungent, the sounds still audible, the experience still acidic. The feelings are less intense now, a little less painful. Putting the stories on paper has helped.

I reconstructed all dialogue and changed the names of nearly all of the non-public people in order to respect their privacy. I was stationed on two Marine fire support bases but I cannot recall either of their names. For simplicity, I have assigned them one name, Fire Support Base Puller. The book also includes a listing of the members of my platoon that I mention in the book, a glossary, and a chronology that lists the main events described in this book against the backdrop of key events that happened throughout the world.

Acknowledgments

No one writes a book alone. So many loving friends guided me in the writing and supported me in the telling of these stories. I am blessed to have them in my life.

Thanks to Olivia, Vince, and Jessica for their professional editing and gentle critique of the final draft. To Rick and Sharon who took the fractured drafts and healed them. Thanks for the helpful comments and support from Larry, Donald, Geoff and Rudayna, Ruth and Rebecca, David and Harriet, and Petr. To my brother, Denny; and friends, Nic, Jim, and Kathy; who shared their experiences at Kent State University, thank you for your courage to relive those thirteen seconds. To my other family members Lynn, David, Sally, Joe, and Florence, who saw me through not only the writing of the book but also the living of the experiences.

To Ingrid for designing the cover. To the librarians at the First Marine Division library and archives at Camp Pendleton for their patience and assistance.

I owe an especially deep debt of gratitude to two Vietnam combat veterans who helped me stay honest: John Young and Rick Reeck. I am proud to call you friends. To the members of my mortar platoon. We kept each other alive in Vietnam—no small feat.

I also wish to honor three World War II veterans who guided me as a soldier and a son: my father-in-law, Bob, my father, James, and my mother, Ruth.

Finally, thank you, Cynthia. The book began in letters to you from a gun pit. Thirty years later, as you held me and listened, you urged me to "write it down." Under your patient, loving tutelage, the stories matured from rough journal entries to this book. It is done now because you taught me how and helped me every step of the way.

Mortar Platoon Members in the Book Including Nickname, Rank, and Primary Responsibility While on Patrol

Platoon Leaders (one per platoon): Cpl. Swenson, "Yale." Replaced Vasquez, sergeant. Command the platoon (total of four guns). Carried personal gear and .45 Cal. pistol.

Forward Observer (one per platoon): "T.J.," corporal. Along with radio operator, seek out suspected enemy positions and target mortar fire. Carried compass, maps, M16 rifle.

Radio Operator (one per platoon): "Long John," corporal. Call in fire missions to the gun crews. Carried PRC-36 radio and .45 Cal. pistol.

Ammo Corporal (one per platoon): "Scrounger," corporal. Secure and maintain all needed supplies. Carried three or four rounds and .45 Cal. pistol.

Section Leaders (two per platoon): "T.J.," corporal. T.J. was formerly the Forward Observer for the platoon. The author replaced T.J. Lead the two mortar sections (two guns each). Carried compass, maps, target plotting board, firing manuals, two or three rounds, and .45 Cal. pistol.

Squad Leaders (four per platoon): "Cowboy," corporal. The author replaced Cowboy. Vulture, corporal. Lead one of the gun crews. Carried gun sight, aiming stakes and lights, three mortar rounds, M16 rifle, and two or more bandoleers of M16 ammunition.

Gunners (four per platoon): "Wild Bill," corporal. Replaced by author and later by Speed. Aimed the guns. Carried bipod, two mortar rounds, M16 rifle, and two bandoleers of M16 ammunition.

Assistant Gunners (four per platoon): "Speed," lance corporal. Replaced by "Crusher," private first class. Drop rounds down the tube. Carried mortar tube, three mortar rounds, M16 rifle, and two or more bandoleers of M16 ammunition.

Ammo Humpers (twelve or more per platoon): Chisholm, "Dutch," Washington, and Ames, all privates first class. Prepare rounds for firing. Carried inner and outer base plate rings, three or more mortar rounds, M16 rifle, and two or more bandoleers of M16 ammunition.

1

Randy: Minneapolis-Saint Paul, Minnesota; February 1996

The Minneapolis Planning Commission meeting ran late, so the 8:00 p.m. 94B bus I caught for home the night I met Randy was not my usual one. The bus was crowded so I sat in the first available seat, next to a large American Indian.

"Vietnam. Randy," was all he said as he stuck out his huge beefy hand, palm down. His breath smelled like stale beer and I pulled my head back a little as I extended my hand. He gripped it and squeezed hard. I squeezed back to avoid pain.

"I'm Michael. I was there too. Where did you serve?"

"Marines. Did you know how hard we took it? Marines were not even twenty percent of the troops, but were thirty percent of the casualties? I am proud to have served my country. You don't find too many people who can say that now."

As we crossed the Mississippi River, he pointed to the stark shoreline, "It reminds me of the Delta, the Mekong Delta." I wondered how the brown landscape frozen by Minnesota's harsh winter could remind him of Vietnam's green lushness.

"I didn't think Marines served in the Delta," I said dubiously.

Undaunted, he replied mysteriously, "I had unique skills." He gesticulated in what looked like sign language. "Anishanaabe. You know, Ojibwe, Chippewa. Communications." His speech alternated between confident, articulated phrases and mumbled monosyllables. "I was responsible for communications. We had another Indian at the other end. Unbreakable codes." I had heard about the famous Indian code-talkers of World War II but did not know about their role in Vietnam. "We could say anything we wanted. The officers never knew," he continued, and then chuckled quietly, lost for a moment.

A pause in the conversation threatened the tenuous connection that bridged the normal social gap between us. Two survivors. I was the first to reconnect. "My mom dealt with codes in the Navy during World War II. She was a 'de-garbler.' Her unit cracked one of the key Japanese naval codes."

Randy was not listening. "Drugs," he said, followed by another long pause. "The war is still very alive for me. The government gave me drugs. I gave me alcohol. The words are in my head but not my mouth. I write poems. I've gone back to the Indian ways," he said becoming more definitive in his sign language.

I asked if he had one of his poems with him. Pointing to his head, he began to recite clear words choreographed by his massive arms and hands. He spoke of the elemental powers of sun and moon, wind and rain, fire, and internal spiritual guidance for truth telling. He said the true spirit of experience needs to come out, "like the rainbow follows the rain." He lost his train of thought and struggled for words, but his hands continued their graceful dance. Cellular memory had not failed him.

"These hands..." his words trailed off as he held his hands out, palms down again, so I could look at them. "I held the hand of my friend just before he stepped on a mine. He was gone and I was left holding his hand. Only his hand. It nearly killed me." I looked hard at him and noticed scars over both eyes, a droopy left eye, a bulbous mis-shapen nose, gray temple hair, and a scar on his chin. He continued, "I think of it every day. Many times a day. That ever happen to you?"

I replied lamely, "I had my share of close calls but came out fine."

Randy asked about my duty and I responded with the basics: 81 mm mortar platoon, Headquarters and Services Company, First Regiment, First Battalion, First Marine Division stationed at Marine fire support bases in the vicinity of Da Nang. "I served a twelve-month tour in '69 and '70."

He went on sporadically, telling stories of government experiments, Agent Orange, his all-Indian communications unit. Then came the pitch: "You gotta' dollar?" I had been so drawn in, his panhandling took me by surprise.

"Sure. You got family?" I asked, beginning to mimic his chopped sentences.

He said he had family coming this weekend from Canada. He repeated his plea, this time softer and more desperate. He said, "I'll be getting off at Wabasha Street so if you...if you want to...you know...."

"Be discrete?" I offered.

"Exactly." His full smile of clean white teeth covered the awkward situation.

I took out my wallet and showed him a picture of my family. As he looked at the picture, I removed a bill and rolled it, magician-like, into the palm of my hand. "Our daughter, Jessica," I said pointing to her, "just left with a friend on a five-month backpacking trip through Europe. I'm very proud of her. She has a wonderful sense of values and a very warm heart. She graduated from a tough college, worked hard, and saved her own money for this trip."

"She is very beautiful," he offered. I told him my wife is a free-lance writer and writing teacher.

"You looked better with a beard," he said pointing at the photo. "Younger." I laughed comfortably.

We got off at different stops in downtown St. Paul. I didn't care what he might do with the twenty. There's a good chance that his

entire story was a well-practiced beggar's scam. There's an even better chance his story is truer than a nonfiction account of the war and
that he's another Vietnam vet like me struggling every day with the
experience.

A few weeks later, I wrote the first of my many pages about the War.

Thanks, Randy.

Semper fi.

2

Toilet Training and Learning to Fly: Parris Island, South Carolina; September 1968

This is my rifle. There are many like it but this one is mine. My rifle is my best friend. It is my life. I must master it as I master my life. My rifle without me is useless. Without my rifle, I am useless. I must fire my rifle true. I must shoot straighter than my enemy who is trying to kill me. I must shoot him before he shoots me. I will....

My rifle is human, even as I, because it is my life. Thus, I will learn it as a brother. I will learn its weaknesses, its strengths, its parts, its accessories, its sights, and its barrel. I will keep my rifle clean and ready, even as I am clean and ready. We will become part of each other. We will....

Before God, I swear this creed. My rifle and myself are the defenders of my country. We are the masters of our enemy. We are the saviors of my life. So be it, until victory is America's and there is no enemy. But Peace!

—Platoon 302 graduation book, Marine Corps Recruit Depot, Parris Island, South Carolina, 1968.

Boot camp was supposed to prepare us for war. I remember the first words from my Chief Drill Instructor, Staff sergeant Martinez, when he boarded the bus that brought a load of fresh recruits including me from the airport at Charleston, South Carolina in the middle of the night.

"On behalf of Major General Ormand R. Simpson, Commanding General of the 1st Marine Division, I welcome you to Parris Island and to Recruit Training Platoon 302." The hint of a smile on his strong narrow face was sucked into a sneer as he continued with a voice like a box of rocks. "Put out your cigarettes. Get rid of your gum. When I say get off my bus, you will hit the street running. You will see cute little yellow footprints on the street. You will find a pair that fits your pretty little feet. **Do you understand!?**"

A few of us said yes.

"When you are given an order here, you will shout 'Yes, sir!' **Do you understand!?**"

"Yes, sir," we responded in unison.

"**I can't hear you, ladies!!**"

"**Yes, sir!!**"

"Now get off my bus you scum bag, scrotum-headed civilians!"

When we had all assembled on the yellow footprints, the first day began. We would not sleep for the next 24 hours.

"From now on I will be your father, your mother, your sister, and your brother. I will be your best friend and your worst enemy. I will be there to tuck you in at night and to kick your ass out of bed in the morning. When I tell you to jump you will ask 'how high.' When I tell you to shit, you will ask 'what color.' Is that clear?"

The Marine Corps had no small task. Staff sergeant Martinez's job was to totally reorder the value systems of impressionable young men. Our screaming "Yes, sir!" was supposed to begin the process.

In order to supply more men to the war, the Marines collapsed their normal twelve-week boot camp training into an especially intense eight weeks that was a totally regimented existence. For sixteen hours a day, seven days a week, our drill instructors pushed our bodies with endless hours of PT (physical training); drilled us in marching, the manual of arms, and hand-to-hand combat; and crammed our minds with the military way of thinking and feeling. Boot camp had two main phases. The first phase was designed to break each individual down through relentless verbal abuse and personal punishment for the most trivial of infractions. Most punishment came in the form of extra PT, typically push-ups, sit-ups and squat thrusts, which we affectionately called "bends and motherfuckers." The second phase had the opposite purpose. The drill instructors rebuilt each of us into an integrated member of the group, the platoon.

Graduation marked the end of the two-stage transformation. The metamorphosis from innocents to "recruits" (creatures only slightly better than the lowest of all forms of life—civilians), and then to soldiers capable of killing the enemy. Not just soldiers, Marines. Boot camp prepared us at least physically and maybe intellectually for this transformation, but not psychologically. Only war itself would do that. Only the first kill.

Instantaneous obedience was a crucial component in the transformation. Staff sergeant Martinez gave us a mixed message on this point. He explained that automatic compliance with orders was critical to a military machine, "but Marines aren't robots. I want thinking Marines." He went on about the Nuremberg Principles, which instruct that soldiers can be found liable for following unlawful orders. However, he qualified this lesson by concluding, "My beloved Corps would never issue an illegal order, so you ladies needn't trouble your pretty little heads over this one."

The drill instructors controlled everything we did, even our visits to the head (toilets). They granted either ten-minute or twenty-minute periods to the entire platoon of sixty men to use the head, depending on whether they wanted us to defecate or not. The extra ten minutes were for "shittin' and gittin.'"

Once, after a ten-minute period, Staff sergeant Martinez inspected the head to look for transgressions and discovered that someone had defecated contrary to orders and had not flushed. This happened during the first phase of training, the demoralizing phase.

"Who shit without permission?" No answer. "I will ask one more time and only once, and one of you slimy douche bags better show me you got a pair and own up to this or you all are going to be in a world of shit. Now who violated my orders and took a dump? When I find the maggot I will rip off his head and shit down his neck!"

Still no confession, so Martinez ordered Private Adams to step forward. Since we were bunked alphabetically, Adams' bunk was closest to the head. "Private Adams!" Martinez roared. "Since not one of you pukes has the balls to admit to this crime, Private Adams here will have to bring the evidence out so the guilty party can identify it as hers. Go get it, Private Adams."

Private Adams, a short but solidly built kid from Mississippi, took on an expression of complete befuddlement. "Sir?" The rest of us breathed a heavy sigh of relief.

Staff sergeant Martinez blared his order a second time into Adams' face, "You heard me, Private shit-for-brains! Go get it and bring it back for the rest of the ladies to see." Adams backed up a half step and froze, still confused. "**Do it! Do it now!**" Adams shuffled off and returned with the sloppy wet turd cradled delicately between his two upturned hands. Sickening ooze dribbled between his fingers and his face cringed as if he was in tremendous physical pain.

With a look of smug satisfaction over his creative genius, Martinez casually gave his next order, "Pass it on."

Pvt. Paul Adams turned to Pvt. Leroy Adams who reluctantly followed orders to accept and pass it on up the alphabet and around the entire squad bay. When Pvt. Brian Jones turned to pass it to Pvt. John Kitson, Kitson stayed at attention, chest out, stomach in, shoulders back, chin up, hands rigid at his side, thumb over the tip of the forefinger. Jones paused a moment, then rotated his hand so the thing slid off and dropped to the floor at Kitson's feet. Almost before it hit with a dull plop, Martinez had stormed half the length of the squad bay and jutted his chin to within two inches of Kitson's face where he launched his verbal attack.

"Who the fuck do you think you are!"

Kitson moved not one millimeter. His eyes fired a return volley directly back into Martinez's gaze.

"Private, are you eye-fucking me?"

"No, sir!" Kitson unfocused his eyes as he was trained.

"Are you some sort of rebel? You think you're a **real** man? Somebody special? Too good for this shit, Kitson?" Martinez fired each taunt with a fine spray of spittle and a bob of his head that drove the stiff brim of his campaign hat into Kitson's forehead. "Speak, worm!"

"No, sir."

"'No, sir' what? No, you're no rebel? We already know that. No you're not a real man? Well, it's my job to make you into one but they don't give me near enough time."

"Sir, the private meant he's not somebody special, sir."

"Damn right! That thing you been passing around came out of one of you ladies. It's no better or worse than any of you. In fact, until I say you can graduate off my island as a United States Marine, I'm not sure which is more valuable. Now, Private Kitson, you **will** pick that thing up like it was your long-lost puppy dog and you **will** pass it on nice and careful like to Private Lantz. Then you will give me fifty push-ups. Now, **do it!**"

Kitson complied. He raced through the push-ups, spurred on by, I thought at first, rage, but then realized it was pride. He had not backed down. It was the appropriate response. Pvt. Puzak passed the thing to me but my mind was more on John Kitson's boldness than on what I held. When Kitson completed his fiftieth pushup, he grunted the obligatory "one more for the Marine Corps" and did one more.

Finally, it came to rest in the quivering hands of Private Alan Zalinski. "Private Zalinski, to the Mirror, front and center." Zalinski stood in front of the barracks's only full-length mirror. A sign taped at the bottom of the mirror read, "This man can be a Marine." "Now, flush that puppy down and haul your ass back here most riki tick."

The exercise made us confront one of the strongest of basic human imprintings—toilet training. Although no pain was involved, passing that turd around was an abhorrent task. In spite of its absurdity, we followed the order and felt disgust not only in the act but also for the cowardly recruit who had disobeyed the pee-only regulation and not owned up to it. The Marine Corps was taking us over right down to our bowels.

Staff sergeant Martinez kept us at attention for a long time. A very long time. Puddles formed to the left and right of our boots from our dripping hands and then dried as quickly as my nose became immune to the ripe odor. Later, little pains began to make their way between my shoulder blades. They scoured a pathway alongside the cords on each side of my neck. They explored my calves for weaknesses. The small of my back began to cry out for attention so I flexed my pelvis back and forth while wriggling my toes to soften the discomfort. The cycle repeated endlessly.

I needed a distraction so I took a mental journey. The pains in my lower back faded from my consciousness as I recalled the prior spring of 1968 when I nearly joined the Navy's aviator training program.

I was walking by a temporary booth at Kent State University, where I was studying architecture. A naval officer was offering a flight in a Navy trainer for anyone who could pass a battery of written tests that evaluated spatial perception. It sounded exciting and I had time between classes so I took the two-hour test. My architecture design training was perfect preparation; I did exceedingly well.

I had dreamed of being a pilot since I was a small boy. I learned to identify scores of World War II aircraft and built plastic models of most of them. As I bicycled out to the University's little airport on the outskirts of town the next morning, the thought of flying in a Navy trainer made me tingle with anticipation. It would be my first flight.

The sun was gaining ground on the cool damp dawn. It was to be a day without clouds. I had no problem finding the right plane and pilot on the little field. There was only one single-engine, prop-driven, World War II-vintage aircraft with Navy insignia emblazoned all over it, and only one man dressed in a uniform to match standing next to it. We shook hands, introduced ourselves and then the pilot, Capt. Strichland, introduced me to the North American T-28C Trojan.

"This model is more advanced than the original 1949 version. She packs a Wright R-1820 power plant with over fourteen hundred horses. We like to call her an engine with two seats strapped on for fun." His speech was slow and very deliberate. Its deep timber reminded me of my father's voice when Dad was in a good mood.

I told him I was surprised to see a prop instead of a jet but he explained this plane could outmaneuver most jets and deliver stresses that could make the best pilots black out.

"She's rated for almost four hundred miles per hour and an altitude of thirty-seven thousand feet but I've pushed her much further than that. Not with students, though," he added with a wry wink and twist of his mouth. He was only two or three years older than my nineteen years, but his disciplined posture and constrained smile betrayed seriousness beyond his years.

"Did you fly missions in Vietnam?"

"Two tours of duty," he said abruptly. That handful of words, I realized later, spoke volumes. Then he directed me to climb up on to the left wing. The plane that looked small and outdated from a distance grew in rich detail as I grabbed the inset handhold and climbed on its wing. The smooth curves of the aluminum skin and its geometric pattern of flush rivets shone with a silvery brilliance as if they were newly sculpted. I peered into the dark cockpit and its two in-line seats and gazed over the flowerbed of dials, levers, switches, handles, pedals, and tiny instruction boxes. Nestled in the middle was a sparse metal seat. It was to be my seat.

"You made it this far with your brains. Now my job is to weed out those who cannot hack movement. Fast, totally disorienting movement. Get in for a ride you'll never forget."

He secured the two sets of straps across my chest and demonstrated how a strike to the center connector freed one set instantly.

"In case of emergency, move this lever up and pull back on the canopy all the way until it locks in the rear position like it is now. Strike that center strap release and climb out on the right wing."

"The right wing…" I mumbled tentatively.

"Yes, the right wing." Again, that reassuring voice. "Have you ever parachuted?"

I said no.

"If you need to on this flight, don't forget to jump between the wing and the rear elevator and don't forget to pull the ripcord. That ring right there."

I fingered the ring and noticed the accelerating rhythm of my heartbeat through it.

"This dial," he said, tapping on the face of the big dial on the upper left of the instrument panel, "this is your airspeed indicator. Now, that big red one on the upper right with two hands is your altimeter." Like the good student, I tapped it as he had just modeled. "Small hand indicates feet above sea level in thousand-foot increments and the larger one in hundreds," he continued. "Now, this one," he tapped the large dial in the center of the panel with the symbol of the airplane suspended in its center, "this is your compass. The big handle by your right leg—the throttle. And that thing between your legs—your control stick."

"We'll be hooked together, right?" I asked.

"My every move will be your every move, and visa versa. Got it?"

"Got it." Although he went on explaining the myriad other lower caste instruments, I absorbed half of what he said, and the other half became aviation fuel for my enthusiasm.

"Fine, we're ready. Put on your helmet and we'll taxi and take off."

He closed my section of the canopy and with a precise surety, climbed into the seat five feet in front of me and disappeared beneath a white helmet.

The white helmet spoke into my ears in a metallic-sounding voice that only resembled that of the man I was entrusting my life to. "Ready to see what this baby can do?"

The engine exploded into life and dominated all else including the "Yeah!" I said excitedly into my helmet's mouthpiece. The plane quaked as the propeller spun itself into a fuzzy disk. The instrument panel awoke and every *needle vibrated in its private circular cage. The powerful radial engine drove a faint perfume of highly refined exhaust into the cabin. The pedals moved my feet back and forth and the stick came alive in my lap to test the reactions of the elevators, stabilizers, and the fin. The throttle moved up and the roar increased in pitch and volume. We taxied into position for the takeoff. I placed my hand on the forward moving throttle and sensed it drive the engine to a fever pitch. G-force pressed me back into the form-fitting seat as we picked up speed, but it could not slow the racing of my heart. In mere seconds, the tricycle landing gear left the ground and nested within the wings and cigar-shaped fuselage. I was airborne for the first time and climbing into a dazzlingly clear blue sky.*

I struggled to clear my ears by pulling on their lobes, yawning, swallowing hard, and moving my jaw from side to side. Just as I succeeded, I heard the voice in my headset: "We own a ten-mile radius of airspace all the way up to 35,000 feet. Let's use it. I'll level us off and I want you to keep us in steady flight on the same heading."

Sure, I've got five minutes experience in the plane and now he wants me to take over. I can't wait.

"Concentrate on keeping the nose about four inches below the horizon and stay to the two-niner-zero heading. Remember, the big dial in the center with the fat little airplane in it?"

I assured him I was ready.

"OK, the stick is yours."

That was it for smooth level flight. The sensitivity amazed me. A move ever so slightly to the left and we began to bank to the left and I slid to the right on the seat. I overcompensated and we rocked the other way and I slid to the left side of the seat. I got the hang of it before I wore out the seat of my pants.

"We're at the edge of our envelope. Here's what a tight left turn feels like."

The pedals moved my feet in opposite directions and the stick jumped to the left and back slightly. G-force pressed down on me again and flattened out my stomach. The horizon smoothly moved perpendicular to the instrument panel as the aircraft pirouetted on its left wing tip. Sunlight played around the inside of the cockpit while the green disk that was the flat top of the world spun to my right. We no sooner completed the turn and righted ourselves than the white helmet said that next would be a snap roll to the right. Like a baton, the horizon twirled 360 degrees to the left around Capt. Strichland's helmet and came to an abrupt stop at the 360th degree—not the 359th nor the 361st. The 360th degree. No other sensation of movement was as apparent as that spinning of the horizon.

"Like that? How about upside down?"

He spun the nose to the right this time 180 degrees. The straps kept my shoulders and waist in place but the powerful gravity from the planet that filled the view "above" me pulled at my legs and feet. Blood and organs oozed into my head and filled the space between my skull and my thoughts. My skin was too tight. A 90-degree snap to the right and we knifed through space on our left side. A final 90 degrees and I checked to confirm that the clouds were appropriately above us and the Earth was appropriately below. Some of my guts still trailed behind on the wake we left in the sky.

My white-helmeted marionette moved the pedals and stick and I was the puppet dancing my way through space. His moves became mine. I wondered if my body was absorbing the lessons better than my mind could figure them out. I dreamed the puppet's dream of cutting the strings.

"The stall. You'll enjoy this…hey, you OK back there?"

"Are you kidding! This is incredible!!" My enthusiasm even surprised me.

"We'll get altitude, then trade that for airspeed in a dive, then we'll…well, you'll see."

He put the plane into a slow climb that simultaneously banked to the right. The ground disappeared and the sun refracted colors among thousands of tiny scratches that ran the length of the canopy. When the altimeter read about 20,000 feet, the stick pushed the nose over.

"This is five or six negative Gs."

The explanation did not stop my stomach from flattening itself against the top of my chest cavity as it continued the climb in spite of the plane's jack-knifing arc toward the ground. Heartbeats pulsed in my eyeballs. Earth replaced sky. My eyes feasted on a huge quilt made of rectangular patches of fresh yellow-green spring growth, criss-crossed by sinuous gray roads and speckled blue jewels of water. I watched the airspeed indicator crank up—260 miles per hour, 280, 300, 340, 390, 450. The Kent State campus grew in the upper part of the canopy. We dove headlong as suicides, and my thoughts accelerated along with the aircraft. Was that Taylor Hall where I had a test in Mechanics of Materials the next day? What's that vibration? Isn't it time to pull up? Isn't this fast enough yet? That's the runway. That's my bicycle!

"That's six or seven positive Gs. Now we go up." The calming voice and positive message in my helmet was an aural balm.

The stick moved slowly to the rear. Taylor Hall and the horizon sank with me into the seat of the airplane. My relative weight doubled, then doubled again, and squeezed the air out of my lungs. A force inside my head threatened to burst my eardrums and crush my head to my chest. The sensation was close to that of diving into the deep end of the pool, only there was no quick relief by swimming back to the surface. The wings shuddered with the stress. They actually rippled. Small aluminum waves slowly washed against the fuselage bluff as we swiped at the runway.

The memory of that compression yanked me out of my meanderings back to the reality of the barracks. My spine and shoulders hurt in the same way. I reassigned the pain. I removed it from the moment and applied it to memory. I needed to fly freely again and found my thoughts back to my first flight, to a time when I at least had the illusion of control.

Looking forward again, Earth and sky changed places a second time. We rode her as two men astride a rocket headed straight up into space. I couldn't help myself. My jubilant scream sounded through my headset, "Yeow!!" I knew I wanted more of this thrill. I wanted the front seat.

Slight adjustments to the stick and pedals and we spun 90 degrees on the tail to place the blinding sun behind our heads. An aerial arabesque. The coordinated movements of two instruments fascinated me. The altimeter climbed back toward our 20,000-foot starting point and the airspeed indicator backed down slowly—240 miles per hour, 180, 120, 80, 40...20. The needle came to rest at the bottom of the dial just as Capt. Strichland switched off the engine. The prop slowed to a stop and the cabin filled with a silence as thick as cold maple syrup.

We sat there, suspended in space. I didn't dare breathe. I didn't want to spoil the moment with movement. Machine, man, motion, and time culminated in a perfect quiet. I felt weightless and delicate as a dandelion blossom gone to seed. From this sublime moment, the plane arched its back like a gymnast and we fell gently back toward Earth and chaos. The pedals and stick began to flop around aimlessly. My marionette relinquished all control and our gentle back flip deteriorated into a spin combined with a roll and a somersault. I could no longer sense any directions. The view through the front of the canopy became a whir of land, sky and a random appearance of the horizon's thin line. Wind whistled by at hurricane speeds. I might have thrown up had I known which way was up. The prop would spin in one direction for a time, then reverse itself. It was as unsure of the situation as I was.

Was this a lesson in trust? Would a sign of distress from me cut off any chance of my qualifying for the next step? Do I parachute from the right or left wing?

"Enjoying the ride?" The question slopped around inside my disoriented head. I could not form an answer. How did he make sense of a world where gravity fights and confuses instead of grounds you? Where up, down, and the ordinal directions tumble like the six faces of a rolled die in a casino.

"Is this better?" The pedals and stick moved simultaneously into new positions and the tumbling horizon unraveled and wrapped itself back around the yellow-green patchwork quilt that held the Earth in place. Again, we were an airplane and crew in a controlled dive.

"Are you forgetting something?" I asked. My words sounded funny, slurred by the taste of stomach bile.

"Oh yes." The engine exploded the silence with its roar. "Thanks. I almost forgot. Say, here's a little twist you may like."

We began to spin on the nose of the plane. Not snap rolls this time. One continuous spin while plummeting toward the ground at ever increasing speed. That one did it for me. Over the edge. It shook my stomach lining off its moorings and it started looking for another place to live. My brain spun inside my head. Whoozy. Dizzy. The stick eased back and the G-force flattened our spin into a crushing pullout.

A pain reawakened in the small of my back and then another behind my knees.

"**Attention!! Drill Instructor on deck!!**" It was Pvt. Zalinski who sounded the alarm that brought me back down to Earth and into the Parris Island barracks of Platoon 302.

"Attention?" screamed Staff sergeant Martinez, as he slapped his swagger stick against trousers that were so perfectly starched and creased they could slice cheese. "You were supposed to be at attention the entire time, assholes." The sergeant could be so endearing. "So what did we learn today, ladies?" he asked with a court jester's lifting of both hands palm up. I answered his rhetorical question by thinking how well I was able to transcend shit, how to float away. Staff sergeant Martinez had a different lesson in mind.

"If one of you fucks up, you all get fucked." Thickly muscled, square-jawed, with rigid posture, Staff sergeant Martinez could have posed for the cover of *Leatherneck* magazine. He strutted the length of the squad bay, voice booming with the righteousness of a televangelist. "You're going to Vietnam, maggots! You screw up over there, you disobey an order, people die. Do you understand?"

"Yes, sir!" The fresh activity was a welcome diversion from the tedium of standing at attention.

"You walk your patrol over there and let your minds drift to some other place for a moment, you might miss the little trip wire stretched across the trail. The mine takes you out and your buddy behind you too." He had reached his stride and the pacing of his speech. "Your little mistake now means four other Marines have to haul your dying asses away and then the Navy has to try to patch you up, or bag and tag your sorry remains and send them home to your mamas." He halted at the front of the barrack, his posture relaxed a little as both hands went to his hips. "I'm glad we had a chance for this little talk this morning." Snapping back to his former disciplined bearing, he concluded his lesson. "Now listen up, recruits. I want this floor so clean you would be happy to eat the mess hall's delicious chow off it. Do you understand?"

"Yes, sir!"

"Make it happen!"

"Aye, aye, sir!"

I had not qualified for the Navy's aviator program. The deteriorating loss of my twenty-twenty vision had already begun. That first flight planted a seed. I knew I wanted the thrill. I knew it had to be a military thrill, a military challenge.

Not long after that first flight, I enlisted in the Marines, a nascent adult of nineteen. A human being in the pupa stage. My drill instructors broke me down within an incredibly short time to a whimpering puppy willing to clean their toilets with a toothbrush. Then they rebuilt me with a new self-image of being physically unlimited, mentally able to use a military model to solve all problems, dedicated to the unquestioning defense of my country, and anxious to test my mettle in Vietnam.

After the eight weeks of grueling training, nearly one quarter of my platoon had washed out of the Marine Corps. They probably would not have survived Vietnam. However, even Marine Corps training could not save three members of Platoon 302. Their names grace the Vietnam Veterans Memorial in Washington, D.C.

Both of my parents drove from Cleveland to attend my graduation, although they knew they would only be able to spend four hours with me. At the culmination of the elaborate two-hour ceremony, Chief Drill Instructor Staff sergeant Martinez stepped forward to be the first to shake our hands and address us by our new titles. No longer recruits, maggots, worms, ladies, or scumbags. Later, I introduced him to my parents and explained to him that both my parents had served in the military during World War II. My father, himself a Marine, knew what I had endured. That day, I looked on all three of them as the parents who had guided me through an initiation rite into one of the most elite fighting forces in the world. I felt a deep pride in my own transformation. I was a Marine.

3

The Wearin' of the Green on the First Day in Hell: Da Nang Airport; March 1969

A big, burly Samurai comes to the wise man and says, "Tell me the nature of heaven and hell." And the Roshi [teacher] looks him in the face and says: "Why should I tell a scruffy, disgusting, miserable slob like you?" The Samurai starts to get purple in the face, his hair starts to stand up, but the Roshi won't stop, he keeps saying, "A miserable worm like you, do you think I should tell you anything?" Consumed by rage, the Samurai draws his sword, and he's just about to cut off the head of the Roshi. Then the Roshi says, "That's hell." The Samurai, who is in fact a sensitive person, instantly gets it, that he just created his own hell; he was deep in hell. It was black and hot, filled with hatred, self-protection, anger, and resentment, so much so that he was going to kill this man. Tears filled his eyes, and he starts to cry and he puts his palms together and the Roshi says, "That's heaven."

—Pema Chodron, *The Wisdom of No Escape and the Path of Loving-Kindness*

We were so young. The average age in Vietnam was nineteen compared to twenty-six for the World War II soldier and 28 for the Korean War. Most Marines I knew were too young to vote, to drink, to sign a legal document, to rent a car, or even to shave. We gave each other nicknames: Vulture, T.J., Scrounger, Wild Bill, Cowboy, Crusher, Dutch, Long John, Speed, and Yale. We wore these aliases to disguise our frightened faces as we saw and did things contrary to our upbringings. We attempted personality makeovers to cope and to try to fit in. We armored ourselves with heavy flak jackets and helmets designed to keep out the red hot shrapnel but not the hot sun. We wore steel-shanked boots of green canvas and black leather, camouflaged uniforms and faces, and carried bristling modern weaponry with steel-hearted macho bravura.

St. Patrick's Day, 1969 fell on a Monday. Instead of green beer and bad jokes, I wore a green uniform and a bad mood. A chartered TWA jet had just carried me the 11,200 miles from San Diego to the bustling tarmac of the Air Force's Da Nang air base with only a three-hour refueling stopover in Hawaii. As part of President Nixon's peace plan to end the War, I helped bring the number of U.S. troops in Vietnam up to its peak of 543,400. I remember taking a moment to savor the crisp, cool modernity of the jet's plush interior as I rose to deplane.

One of the crewmembers, a petite blonde, stood close to the doorway. "Good luck, Marine," she said with a genuine smile, the last I would see on an American woman for a year. I stepped into the doorway and an intensely bright panorama of Vietnam embraced me. The sauna-level heat and humidity quickly squeezed the breath and sweat out of me.

All of the former passengers, easily two hundred Marines originating from various States-side units, huddled together amidst swirling clouds of fine glistening dust to play the all-too-familiar "hurry up and wait" game. Eventually, we were marched to a shadeless area in front of the supply depot and ordered to form up. It was the sloppiest formation of my short military career because we were all woozy from jet lag and the sun's assault.

"I chose this?" I thought to myself. I recalled the day of my last arrival on a Marine base. It was three weeks earlier at Camp Pendleton near Oceanside, California. The weather was dreamily perfect that February afternoon but the troop truck ahead of mine disgorged a unit of Marines dressed in all white, winter weather clothing. I learned that they had spent a week in the low mountains to the east in winter warfare training. A month earlier, the North Koreans had captured the U.S.S. Pueblo and its Navy crew under the charge of trespassing and spying in North Korean waters. We were merely getting ready for the usual response: Send in the Marines.

The next day our Commanding Officer announced that orders were changed and my unit was to begin winter warfare training in two days. My heart sank. After training for six months to handle the difficulties of a guerilla war in the tropical climate of a primitive developing country, I shuddered to think of the difficulties of fighting a modern military force in the North Korean winter. I flashed on the Korean War photos I had seen of soldier's fingers frozen around their M1 rifles, and haggard, black-and-white faces iced with frost that glowered from under blanketed helmets. I was ready for 120 degrees, not thirty below; green jungle boots, not white bunny boots; dysentery, not frostbite; peasants planting punji stakes and land mines, not trained soldiers flying Migs and driving tanks. Unit morale plummeted until the following day when the CO announced that plans had changed again. No winter survival training, "You're all going to Vietnam." A cheer burst from each of us. "Yea! We're going to Vietnam."

As I stood on that Da Nang tarmac, flies swarmed around my face in search of the sweat that ran in rivulets from my scalp and then formed tributaries around the potholes of my bloodshot eyes. I wondered if there was one psychological warfare unit whose job it was to dress up in winter survival gear as an elaborate setup for each Marine company arriving at Pendleton on their way to Vietnam.

About an hour later, a deeply tanned supply clerk, dressed in a crisply starched and pressed uniform, issued me the essentials for my new job:

• A heavy mottled-gray helmet with chin strap, a plastic helmet liner, and cotton camouflaged cover. Later, I would develop a technique of using this helmet as a crude boiler to make my squad fruit cobbler from combat rations (C-rats). I would sit on it, use it as a pillow and a sink, decorate it with a peace sign, and, one day, use it as a club to chase off the deadly, iridescent-green bamboo viper snake I nearly sat on.

• An olive drab flak jacket with an inside label that cautioned: "Wear this jacket; it may save your life." I would wear it. In fact, I would wear it out completely by the end of my tour of duty. Although some of its heavy plastic armor plates eventually worked their way out of rips, which reduced its effectiveness, I wore it proudly. Its dull ragged cloth, bearing my nickname inscription, "J. M.," across the back in faded black letters, would come to signify the dignity of survival—the greatest accomplishment Vietnam offered.

• Jungle boots, one pair. They had a steel backbone in the sole to protect against the punji stakes the enemy used in the early years of the War. By 1969, the enemy relied more on mines that would explode under the boot and exploit its steel shank for additional shrapnel. I would wear holes in these boots in less than four months of stomping through sand and rock, jungle and mud. During the three months of monsoon, both my boots and feet would rot from never being dry. Replacement boots were so hard to come by, Marines rotating home would bequeath them to those remaining behind.

• An M16 Armalite assault rifle, complete with sling, cleaning kit, and a cloth bandoleer of magazines already loaded with 18 rounds each. No other object in my life up to that time or since has captured more of my attention and care. My rifle and I struck a bargain. I would maintain it meticulously and it would never jam on me. I would keep it close and it would give me a sense of security. I would strike a John Wayne pose with it for snapshots and aim it into tree lines and at anything that moved. It would fire 5.56 mm high-powered ammunition at the rate of eight hundred rounds per minute at any target I wished. It made me powerful and dangerous. It was never further than an arm's length away until I turned it in on this same base one year later. Like my boot camp rifle prayer, we became "part of each other." I have not fired a rifle since.

On that first day in Vietnam, my new equipment just added to the heavy anxiety I had awaiting orders. Hours later, another snappily dressed clerk shouted my name and handed me a single piece of paper assigning a "Private First Class James M. Orange, 2479060, MOS 0341," to Fire Support Base Puller.

"They'll be happy to see you. Lots of KIAs there," he said, referring to Marines killed in action. "Now get in that jeep over there. Move it! They're ready to leave."

The passenger seat next to the driver was already taken by another new arrival. Like me, he wore heavy sweat-stained cotton utilities and had the same look of bewilderment, fear, and exhaustion. I clambered up on the rear deck of the oversized jeep and it immediately sped off as if my arrival was the only thing delaying departure. As we raced off the air base, I pulled on my flak jacket and helmet while struggling to stay clear of the standing Marine who kept swinging a post-mounted M60 machine gun from side to side. For body armor, he had only cracked jungle boots, a faded pair of green shorts, and a helmet decorated with the adage "GET SOME" painted with dirty white letters that were barely visible against the camouflaged cloth helmet cover. His darkly tanned and finely wrinkled skin was shrink-wrapped around a tall, sinewy frame.

Nausea crept up from my gut. At first, I thought it was from the heat, the jerking ride, and weariness from the long sleepless flight, but I soon realized it was loneliness. Bouncing around on the back of that jeep, I recalled the similarities with my first endless day in boot camp—the stifling South Carolina summer heat; the exhaustion from lack of sleep; the sense of being friendless. Eventually, during those eight weeks of training and abuse, I became part of a small group of friends who had endured it with me. However, subsequent training assignments over the next five months winnowed the group down. On the flight to Nam, only one member of my boot camp platoon was with me, John Kitson. He drew a different base assignment and I never got the chance to wish him well. Decades later, I would find his name among 58,000 others on a polished black granite wall in Washington, D.C.

No one spoke a word during the entire two-hour trip as we bounced and weaved along the pot-holed road that threaded its way between verdant rice paddies tended by peaceful-looking farmers in conical straw hats. Then the road snaked into a thickening jungle that screened the light from the waning sun but trapped its thermal power like a greenhouse. I snapped a magazine into my jet black M16 and peered into the tangled brush like a fortune teller trying to divine the future from a cup full of tea leaves.

We emerged into an expansive clearing and approached the fire support base. It was located about twenty miles southeast of Da Nang in northern Quang Nam Province and a few miles from Hill 55, which I only recently learned was named Camp Muir, the Vietnam headquarters for the First Marine Division.

Barbed concertina wire encircled the base like a sparkling silver curtain of lace. Two hunkering, sand bag bunkers with dark slits for windows separated the wire just enough for the road to penetrate. As we drove through this break in the outer perimeter defenses with hardly a reduction in speed, I turned back to see the guards, neither of whom paid any attention to us. Fifty yards further in, we came upon two more bunkers that formed a gateway through the more extensive inner perimeter defenses. They were identical to the last and were manned by equally uninterested sentries leaning on their M60s and smoking. What I saw of the base as we drove toward the 81 mm mortar platoon area located at its south end struck me as an odd hodgepodge of tents and low, single-storied sandbag buildings seemingly slapped together and scattered about. Here everything bustled. Marines were busy with all the tasks of living, playing, and war-making.

Our vehicle came to an abrupt halt, creating a small cloud of fine yellow dust, and the driver spoke his first words while looking in the rear view mirror mounted on the front hood: "You, in the rear, get out."

I complied like a canine graduate just out of obedience school and just stood there as the jeep left with the other new replacement. A boisterous volleyball game drew my attention. At first, it amazed me anyone would voluntarily run, jump, and aggressively compete in the oppressive heat. Then I noticed no one was obeying normal rules of play. Points and take-overs seemed to be accorded based on who protested the loudest. I later learned there was only one rule for Vietnam volleyball—the "jungle-rule." It meant no rules. Eventually, my new Platoon Leader, Sgt. Vasquez, paused the game long enough to grant me a warm greeting and introduction to the rest of the platoon. He was overweight, covered in black body hair, and dressed only in shorts and boots. "Hey, fresh cheese! Another FNG!" This was no term of endearment. FNG was short for "fucking new guy."

Since I was still dressed in heavy khaki utilities, he directed me to a pile of light-weight jungle fatigues over near the base perimeter. The dank stench rising from the mound of clothes added to my heat-and-jet-lag induced dizziness. Then I noticed the holes and rips. The blood stains. This was my first lesson in the difficulties of supply.

Before the thought could roil my stomach, something cracked faintly by the right side of my head and added more holes to the camouflaged shrouds. Then another crack sounded by the left side of my head, this one close enough that I recall its Doppler-affected, miniature sonic boom. First day. First sniper. First dive for cover. I burrowed mole-like into the clothing and achieved my best ever job of concealment. Within seconds, return fire from a dozen places all around me silenced the shooter.

After I stopped shaking, I returned to the task of shopping for an outfit. I found trousers and a shirt that were a perfect fit. The tunic top had one little hole with a small stale-red stain just to the left of the second button from the top.

I would wear a dead man's clothes.

4

A Study in Change and Motion: Marine Fire Support Base Puller; April 1969

Strangely, such horrifying memories [of the carnage of war] seem to have a much more profound effect on the combatant—the participant in battle—than the non-combatant, the correspondent, civilian, [prisoner of war], or other passive observer of the battle zone. The combat soldier seems to feel a deep sense of responsibility and accountability for what he sees around him. It is as though every enemy dead is a human being he has killed, and every friendly dead is a comrade for whom he was responsible. With every effort to reconcile these two responsibilities, more guilt is added to the horror that surrounds the soldier.

—Lt. Col. Dave Grossman, *On Killing: The Psychological Cost of Learning to Kill in War and Society*

The thirty-foot elevation of a guard tower in Vietnam offered a long view: A view beyond the two barrack tents that housed my 81 mm mortar platoon and the platoon's four gun pits. A view beyond the

27

bomb-cratered rice paddies that lay between our perimeter defenses and the quiet little village five hundred yards distant. A view that encompassed the entire Marine fire support base in the middle of Quang Nam Province, over one hundred miles from the Demilitarized Zone (DMZ) and half a world away from my home.

Our firebase had seven towers. From my perch in Guard Tower Number 2, I could see Guard Towers Number 3 and 1. Number 3 was to my right and southwest about seventy yards. Number 1 was about the same distance to the north and located adjacent to the camp entrance. The three towers framed the curving eastern edge of the firebase. Odd-numbered towers had two guards with an M79 grenade launcher, an M60 machine gun, and, occasionally, an M72 rocket launcher. Even-numbered towers had a lone Marine and his rifle.

I had a good view of the village and its rice fields. On that day new rice stalks, less than a foot high, painted the paddy steppes a bright pea-green color that contrasted with the iron-red of the clay paddy walls. A water buffalo pulled its plow and lone farmer through the muck of the uppermost paddy. In the village, bent old women, teeth blackened from chewing betel nuts, a few old men, and dozens of kids lived in the shanties and thatched-roof huts. It was a scene as timeless as an ancient dragonfly caught in amber. As familiar as I was with its look and rhythms, I never learned the village's name.

Able-bodied young men were conspicuously absent. No doubt they had already been conscripted by one of the three branches of the Vietnamese military: the Army of the Republic of Vietnam (ARVN), our allies; the North Vietnamese Army (NVA); or the insurgent Communist forces of the National Liberation Front, better known as Viet Cong, VC, or Victor Charley, our enemy.

The razor sharp edges of the double rows of spiraling concertina wire glistened in the midday sun. I had strung what seemed like miles of this stuff around our base and had the cuts to prove it. More experienced Marines had booby-trapped the perimeter wire with trip flares and Claymore mines. Each mine packed seven hundred ball bearings imbedded in a plastique shape charge designed to make literal mincemeat of intruders.

Inside the perimeter defenses and near the base's entrance and Tower Number 1, some Vietnamese from the village ran a tailor shop and a barber shop, and sold things like film, toothpaste, radios, and other black market goods out of a rickety shack. It barely offered shelter from the sun's penetrating beam and the incessant rain of the monsoon season. In boot camp, Staff sergeant Martinez never told us Vietnamese would be on the firebases or that they would cut our hair and launder our clothes.

Kids often rummaged through our trash barrels there for food or cloth to repair the rags that hung on their little bodies. A scrap of cardboard, wood, or plastic made their ramshackle huts a little more resilient. I had never seen this degree of destitution. "Don't trust any gooks," Martinez had warned us with passionate disgust. He survived two tours of duty in Vietnam, so I had listened to him studiously.

I stepped to the rear of the guard tower and I followed the movements of my fellow Marines below. Only two things drove soldiers from the shade on one hundred-degree scorchers like this one. I chuckled as I watched the unlucky ones fill sandbags and burn shit. Empty fifty-five-gallon drums cut in half served as our septic tanks. When full, we pulled them away from the bottoms of the outhouses, added diesel fuel and toilet paper, and then stirred the twenty gallons of gumbo gingerly for a few minutes to get a smooth consistency prior to lighting it up. The ever-present odor became the signature of base camp.

Having completed a 360-degree visual reconnaissance, I rechecked my M16. Locked and loaded with eighteen rounds of high-powered ammunition with the nineteenth round already in the chamber, selector switch on SAFE, windage on the rear sight set on zero. Half out of boredom, half for the sake of perpetual practice, I swung it up and seated it deep into my right shoulder. Right elbow high, I rotated my left elbow into my rib cage and trained the sights on a rock out beyond the concertina wire. "Bone support," Martinez preached. "Be the bone equivalent of a tripod." In boot camp, he taught me to intertwine my rifle sling so tightly around my left arm and wrist I felt the weapon had grafted itself to my frame. After countless hours in painful firing positions with an empty rifle, the only reward was the repetitive dull "click" of the hammer. The consummate experience of boot camp was the rifle range. Firing live rounds at the human-shaped silhouettes on paper targets engaged all my senses and resulted in my marksmanship award. Alone in Guard Tower Number 2, I had graduated to the next stage where both the rounds and the targets were live and the reward was survival.

I squeezed off an imaginary round into the forehead of the rock, sat down on the upended ammo crate and turned my attention to *Calculus and Analytic Geometry*, by George B. Thomas Jr., the text for the correspondence course I was taking. At that time, early in my tour of duty, I still harbored the long-term view of a normal post-Vietnam world for myself.

Calculus was one of the reasons for my being in Vietnam. It was a requirement for the architecture degree I was working on at Kent State University in Ohio, but I did so poorly in it I ended up on academic probation and lost my college deferment at the end of the 1967 school year. My Cleveland draft board was about to reclassify me as "Class I-A: Registrant available for military service."

I did have choices. I could concentrate on my studies or change majors (and dreams) if necessary to dodge or at least postpone the draft. Ironically, I did change my major after returning to school upon being discharged. Canada was also an option; ten thousand U. S. draft dodgers sought safe asylum there during the war. Or, I could stay and fight the draft and risk a prison sentence; nearly two hundred fifty thousand young American men did resist the draft laws during the War. Declaring myself a conscientious objector (CO) was not an option at the time of my enlistment. Only Quakers and Jehovah's Witnesses could get CO status because both religions had long histories of pacifism and consistent opposition to all wars. Later, CO status was available to those who could effectively argue that they weren't opposed to all wars, but only the Vietnam War. I even helped a friend draft his application in 1971 after I returned home. He was successful.

I had choices, but in the summer of 1967, I was still a patriot at heart. I was the product of the hero myths of my youth. I had absorbed the messages from my Catholic faith that condemned "godless Communists" and from the Hollywood formula movies that glorified World War II. When President John F. Kennedy proclaimed during his Inauguration Day speech in 1961 that America would "bear any burden, meet any hardship, support any friend, and oppose any foe to assure the survival and success of liberty," I, like so many others in my generation, felt a deep stirring of romantic patriotism. "Ask not what your country can do for you, ask what you can do for your country" is still the single most memorable sentence of my life. It resonated perfectly with the altruistic ideals I learned from my church and parents. In 1965, I argued for increased U.S. involvement in Vietnam in a high school debate. That same summer, I visited the Lincoln memorial in Washington, D.C. and wept at Lincoln's eulogy to the fallen soldiers at Gettysburg, engraved on the memorial's polished white marble.

I envied the moral certitude of my parents' world that had been shaped by the "Good War." Instead of their black-and-white views, I faced an ambiguous blur of contradictory concepts, confusing events, and difficult questions: The Domino Theory; containment of Communism; treaty commitments with the nascent South Vietnamese government; searing images of the Buddhist monks immolating themselves in protest of the oppressive Diem regime, our puppet dictator; the August 1964, Tonkin Gulf incident. The political issues of the era nagged at my conscience: Was this a war of national liberation? Were we fighting on the wrong side? Was it a civil war being used as a proxy for the Cold War? Were North Vietnam and its allies waging a war of aggression? Was Ho Chi Minh a nationalist hero or a Southeast Asian Stalin? Was it wise to step in where the French left off? How could fighting, killing, and risking death be compatible with my values and dreams? How would I prefer to enter manhood: as a Vietnam vet or as a draft dodger? I lacked the conviction and courage to resist the draft and I could not shirk my duty in good conscience. Becoming a man meant becoming a soldier.

I have long hated the concept expressed by the phrase "fuck it." It predicts a temporary suspension of reason and ethics, a personal surrender. In Nam, otherwise reasonable people said "fuck it" and opened up on automatic on any target. In the summer of 1968, I said, "fuck it" and joined the Marines. The Marines promised to make a man out of me and offered the shortest time in uniform—eighteen months of active duty. The thought of the GI Bill to help finance school after the service sounded very good. I was having a hard time working my way through college. The mindless job in the military of simply taking orders looked a lot easier than succeeding in architecture school.

I shaved my head the night before I shipped out for six months of training: Boot camp at Parris Island, South Carolina; Advanced Infantry Training School and Mortar School at Camp Geiger in Charlotte, North Carolina; and final training in Camp Pendleton near Oceanside, California. By March 1969, I was in excellent physical shape, trained to kill and willing to die for my country. Then my Commander in Chief, President Richard M. Nixon, sent me to Vietnam to put my new skills and sense of purpose to the test.

Back in Guard Tower Number 2, the text on my lap beckoned: Calculus, the study of change and motion. As I had done at Kent State just months earlier, I again struggled to calculate the distance between two points via a series of estimates of the halfway point. The more numerous the estimates, the greater the precision. Even though the dichotomy of mathematics' exactness was in stark contrast to the War's uncertainties, the calculus technique of getting from point A to B by multiple halfway measures seemed ironically consonant with the series of decisions I made, each bringing me halfway to where I was sitting at that moment.

My mind wandered again and so did my gaze. About thirty yards directly to the west, I noticed two boys rummaging through a garbage can located next to one of Charley Company's barrack tents. It was unusual for Vietnamese to wander this far from their shack by the base entrance. The boys looked about eight and ten years old. They were both frail and emaciated. Our garbage was their feast.

With a start, they raced away from the garbage can back toward the base entrance. In a couple of seconds, a crunching, bone-crushing explosion punched my tower. The blast and the shrapnel it fashioned from the garbage can shredded the barrack tent's wooden platform floor and contents, and heaved the burning mass into the air atop a dark sphere of smoke that rode a core of yellow flame. The shock wave knocked the two kids to the ground momentarily. I quickly surmised they had planted a home-made bomb but it had a fuse that was too short.

Instinctively, I traded tools, dropped *Calculus and Analytic Geometry*, and grabbed the pistol grip of my M16 while assuming the standing firing position. I thumbed the selector off SAFE, past SEMI and all the way over to AUTO as I shouldered the weapon, oblivious as to whether the target was another paper silhouette from the rifle range or a young boy. The constant drills by Staff sergeant Martinez came alive in my head. "Snap in. Aim in. Breath control. Focus on the front sight post, not the target." Only on the rifle range did the drill Instructor ever use a soothing voice. His coaching was as meditative as a Zen centering exercise. "Keep it to three-round bursts. The up-and-left pull of the M16 will waste the Marine Corps' fourth round." Through the circular rear sight, I saw the target do a running dance between the front sight post and the left edge of the front sight as I lead him. I recalled the firing range adage: aim low when firing down. My chest muscles had already halted their bellows action. "If you're squeezing that trigger oh so slowly," advised Martinez, "you won't know when the hammer is released. Learn to make that moment happen between your heartbeats or you'll never get off my rifle range." His relentless training had set me on the same automatic fire as my weapon.

A three-round burst erupted from the machine gun to my north in Tower Number 1. The gunner had a clear shot at less than twenty yards of the two boys as they ran directly toward him. The fine dust danced a three-step toward the taller and faster boy. The next burst ripped through his right thigh, belly, and chest and sent him reeling. An instant later, after a minute adjustment by the gunner, three more lead slugs, rocketing at Mach 3, bore clean through the chest of the smaller trailing boy. He collapsed abruptly in a heap not more than three feet from the other boy. Then I heard the heavy metallic, jack hammer sounds from the other machine gunner in Tower Number 3. A moment later, came the higher-pitched reports of M16 fire and the small area around the boys became a free-fire zone.

In boot camp, Staff sergeant Martinez described in detail how the 5.56 mm M16 round was designed to be just enough off-balance so it would tumble after entering soft flesh. I had studied the complex trajectory of an imbalanced object as a practical example in my calculus course. In the textbook case, it was a tossed hammer. Now I was observing this equation in terms of hot metal tossed through little boys.

The two boys came apart in the firing frenzy. Sound reverberated from all directions for an interminable time as the metal opened them up, exploded their faces, and spilled their intestines onto the reddening sand. They no longer looked human; more like freeway road kill when the evisceration is so severe you cannot identify the species. I stared, but could not fire. Targets no longer, I saw only dead children.

I do not remember what happened to the boys' bodies. I do not remember what happened to the three Charley Company Marines who were resting in the hooch before the explosion. I vaguely remember hearing low moans and cries for a medic, seeing blackened and bleeding bodies. A medevac chopper probably arrived within minutes to whisk them to a hospital ship moored in the South China Sea, but I cannot be sure.

I do remember wondering how parents could send their children on a suicide mission. I admired the intensity of their dedication if not their methods. Their mission succeeded. Days later, we learned that two of the wounded Marines had died. I realized the Vietnamese were fighting for their land, for their next meal, for their lives. For them, war was a life-long, inter-generational, noble endeavor. For me, the War had become little more than a job. I had joined it with confused motives that included both patriotic duty and a subconscious need for a male right of passage. Two dead boys—the first of many deaths I would witness during my tour of duty—taught me what was at stake.

The incident with the two boys was easier for me to live with because I did not pull my trigger. Others did the killing. But this I know, if the incident had occurred just one month later after I had experienced my first search and destroy missions and patrols to find the bodies destroyed by my mortar rounds, my bullets would have been the first to rip the boys to shreds. Although I did not pull my trigger then, their two faces are among so many others that haunted my dreams.

I never picked up that calculus book again.

5

Fire in the Hole: Fire Support Base Puller; April 1969

And it's 1,2,3, what are we fighting 4? Don't ask me I don't give a damn. Next stop is Vietnam. And it's 5,6,7, open up the Pearly Gates. Well there ain't no time to wonder why. Whoopee we're all going to die!

—Country Joe and the Fish, "I-Feel-Like-I'm-Fixin'-to-Die Rag."

"Take it in, man. Drag it down deep. Hold it in now. That's it, man. OK, let it out slow and feel the weight come off. You're off duty and on to something now, man. You got it now, man. Smokin' Nam grass is the only way to beat this war. The **only** way, slick."

I opened my eyes to peer through my thick exhalation of smoke and saw in the pale suggestion of the Vietnamese moonlight the huge grin of Cpl. William Trapinski, "Wild Bill." His deeply creased face and prominent nose drifted away as the euphoria inflated me like a slowly drifting balloon in a Macy's parade. A virgin to marijuana, I eased myself back against the gun pit wall at a minute-hand's pace and looked upwards into the innocent, star-glinted heavens.

"Whoa, Jack, come on back" Wild Bill advised. "Tell me Whuzhappenin. Don't Bogart that joint, man. You got plenty of time to toke on the weed. You got 3-6-5 and a wake-up before you can la dai outta' here."

I passed him the Marlboro-sized joint, expertly rolled by the local Vietnamese, and he offered me his Camel in return.

"I don't smoke," I said.

"You will. Hell, they give you four free cigs in every other C-rat package." He took a quick hit and continued. "Dig this. There's got to be one cigarette for every joint. You see anyone you don't know or trust approach you, you douse the joint, shitcan it and take a puff on the lit cigarette."

"Why?" I asked dreamily (there's a reason the stuff is called "dope").

"Well, picture this scene, you and me right here, but from the perspective of the officer who'd love to bust your ass to the brig in Japan for smokin' grass. From a distance, he sees a couple of guys smoking something. When he's up close, he needs to see a lit cigarette. Now you get it?"

"Yeah," I said. "Pass me that Camel. It's true, marijuana does lead to harder drugs."

Wild Bill taught me how to cup my hand around the lit end to hide its glow. How to open and ignite a Zippo lighter with a finger snap. How to slowly inhale a fifty/fifty mixture of smoke and air with an exaggerated hiss. How to lose myself in the illusion of peacefulness. How to create a safe place full of meaning, music, and humor. How to feel good in an insane world.

His leathery face and premature balding disguised the fact that less than two years earlier he was a teenager living a carefree life as an apprentice carpenter in Lexington, Kentucky. His gaunt body concealed his ability to carry his own weight of 120 pounds in armaments all day through the glue-like mud of a Vietnamese jungle. His friendship became a life preserver when I was engulfed in a sea of fear and loneliness at the beginning of my tour of duty. He had honed a personality that was a combination of '50s beatnik and Indian guru. His alert, squinting eyes absorbed everything around him without letting it affect his centered calm. Often, when he hunkered down behind the sand bag walls of the gun pit, we kidded him for looking Vietnamese.

By the time I arrived, Wild Bill already had nine months in country and was replete with survival skills earned under heavy fire in Operations Meade River and Dewey Canyon. Hungry to learn of his battle experiences, I tried to glean details from him about the operations. He named two people, then paused long with a downcast gaze and a shake of his head. The fingers of both hands combed through the too-short stubble that survived on the sides of his head. I pressed him and all he said was "Dead. And for what? Dewey fucking Canyon?" I read later that Operation Dewey Canyon came to be known as one of the most significant American victories of the War, but it came at a terrible price in American dead and wounded. Wild Bill was even more tight-lipped about his life back home.

"The whores here just do nothing for me but bring me down." I was caught off guard by Wild Bill's out-of-the-blue comment. "Have you fucked the village whores yet?"

I replied in the negative. As if to redeem my standing in his eyes, I told him about my visit to Tijuana two weeks before flying to Vietnam. On leave from Camp Pendleton, California, I took the bus with two other Marines to the famous Mexican border town to see what I could see.

The bus dropped the three of us at the border gate at about 8:00 p.m. and we crossed over and walked the quarter mile into the heart of the teeming city. Within minutes a Mexican youth who hung out at a dark intersection offered an experience that, for some inexplicable reason, was irresistible to my two companions: "Hey, Marines, you want to see a donkey fuck a woman?" While my friends and I exchanged theories about how the kid had deduced we were Marines considering we were in civilian clothes, the teenage barker reeled us in with the promise that he would give us a special treat. "All three of you come to the show and I'll let you fuck my sister. She's a virgin."

More nervous titters disguised our uneasiness while we considered how this would certainly be a unique experience. With a wave of his hand, the kid beckoned a taxi from a murky back street. My two companions climbed in. I started for the door but recalled the sole word of warning from our Company Commander before we left: "Do not take a taxi in Tijuana. You lose control the moment you enter the car." I hesitated.

"Come on," my friends urged me. "If you wimp out on us, we'll lose the special deal on the virgin." The barker must have seen the doubt in my eyes because he signaled the taxi to leave and then called after it "Tell my sister I said hi."

I walked to the nearest bar wondering if I had somehow missed some exotic wonder of the world, and took a seat at a small table near the open doorway. The place had a wide U-shaped bar with the open end anchored to the back wall and a sole barmaid on the inside who tended to the twenty or so men seated around it. Before I could sort out the intermingled smells of tobacco smoke, perfume, alcohol, and urine, a waitress took my drink order for a Mexican beer. The place was filled with swarthy men and tawny women wreathed in smoke and low talk. Soft Mexican music oozed from the speaker system. A few minutes later, a woman at least ten years my senior and twenty pounds heavier brought my beer and nonchalantly sat on my lap. She leaned forward towards me so I could peer down into her ample bosom and then she planted a tobacco-tainted kiss on my cheek. "You like to buy me a drink?" I did. Within seconds, a small glass of clear liquid appeared on the table and a boy no older than ten demanded five dollars. As I pealed off the bill from the roll I kept in my sock, the music shifted to something dark and sultry. All the men seated around the U-shaped bar sat up straighter on their stools, pulled their drinks and ashtrays closer, and reached for their wallets.

"You'll like this," my new best friend said as she squirmed on my lap to get a better view. The lights dimmed and, at the far end of the bar, an undersized door opened out of the wall at the same height as the top of the bar. A ceiling spotlight cut the haze for a young dancer who emerged clad in a white bikini costume and a simple black mask that covered only her eyes. Her supple body was a feast for my hungry eyes as she writhed slowly to the music atop the gentle curve of the bar. I reached for my beer and the woman on my lap told me to watch what happens next.

The dancer began the striptease. With only two items of clothing, it didn't take long, but she slowed it down with her delicious skills. When a man seated at the bar ten feet from me slapped a bill down on the bar top, the spotlight shifted to it and she danced her way there. A strobe light kicked in as she straddled the bill and the man's upturned smile. In synch with the slow grinding throb of the music, she lowered herself onto his face, wrapped her legs around his ears, and reached down behind her for the bill. As her body wriggled, the entire bar broke into wild applause. Me too. The customer's time was up. With methodical precision, she proceeded to make her way around the entire bar top face by face, bill by bill.

"What did you do?" asked Wild Bill.

"Nothing. I finished my beer, tipped the hooker in my lap and walked back over the bridge to the border where my bus was waiting."

"Hell, you pass up the donkey show, the free virgin, the lap whore, and the face plant. What are you waiting for, true love?" His question had just the right hint of sarcasm.

"I suppose."

Wild Bill and I shared another long draw on the joint and sank into an equally long pause in the conversation. After a time, I took his quietness as an invitation to talk about my true love. The woman I left back home, Bridget. I started my story in the fall of 1967 at a wedding in Galion, Ohio. One year before I went to boot camp. I told him how I felt trapped the moment I first saw her. Blonde hair sashayed across the middle of her back as she walked past my table to join the food line at the wedding reception. Her long blue dress repeated a wavy sculpture of shoulders, waist, and hips. Coordinated blue spiked heals forced an athletic flexing and relaxing of definitive calf muscles. She rewarded my strained over-the-shoulder gawk with a turn of her head that exposed a thin face and high cheekbones. Her peripheral vision must have picked up on my stare because she turned her head fully to meet my eyes. A slight, one-sided smile shot a shiver down my spine and her eyes lingered. I had to have her.

I passed him the sole snapshot of Bridget I carried with me in a sealed baggie. Wild Bill took a long look in the weak light. The full-length close-up of her showed golden late afternoon sun back-lighting her. "Nice," was all he had to say. His head nodded in agreement as he passed the photo back to me.

Now completely relaxed, I picked up the one-sided conversation by sharing my dilemma, a second woman. "You're not 'gonna believe this, man, but it's the truth," I started. "Her name is Cynthia and I met her last July on the observation deck at the top floor of the Empire State Building."

"The Empire State Building? No shit?"

"No shit." I may have been green to Vietnam, but I was gaining some status as a romantic. I told my friend, Wild Bill, about the turmoil and change of that summer of 1968. I described the trouble in architecture school, the trouble in my relationship with Bridget, and my snap decision to enlist. With the war temporarily on hold that night, I took my time heaping detail upon detail to paint the full picture of the influences that shaped that summer. "My head was spinning, Wild Bill, so I joined a few old buddies from the seminary on a trip to New York City. We stayed in this dump of a hotel, the Broadway Central, and..."

"Whoa. Say again about the 'seminary,' Jack."

"St. Charles Borromeo Seminary in Cleveland. That's where I went to high school."

"Now you're really tripping me out, man." Wild Bill said. "You're a fucking priest?"

"Hell no. It's just that when I was 13, I thought I had a vocation to become a priest so I went to this seminary to study. I dropped out after my high school graduation and then went to architecture school at Kent State University."

"What the hell are you doing in the Marines?" Wild Bill had to ask the obvious question. I had no obvious answer and Wild Bill did not wait for one.

"So, let's see if I got this straight. You went to a seminary to become a priest, quit that idea, then went to college to become an architect, fell in love with this blonde, and then dropped the school and the blonde so you could come here and drop mortars on people? Oh, yes, plus you got a second girlfriend that you met at the top of the Empire State Building? Have I got it right."

"Basically."

"You survive your tour of duty, you're gonna' need to get some help to sort this out when you get back or you will definitely be totally freaked out, man." He took a drag on the joint, passed it back to me, and continued. "I want you to lay this story on me about this New York woman and then I'm going to tell you something."

I jumped at the invitation and explained that I had been traveling with three friends, former high school classmates who, like me, had left the seminary two years earlier. My group noticed Cynthia and her two friends. We approached. "Only door-knocking Mormons could have looked safer than we four ex-seminarians." As our two groups merged and huddled, the normal awkwardness of first meetings melted quickly. We all agreed to go together to the Village to hear some music. By the time we began our walk down 42nd St., Cynthia and I paired up in a private conversation that did not end until I saw her off at JFK Airport late the next afternoon.

I described how Washington Square and Greenwich Village were vibrant with the music and bar scene, and the heated political discussions that percolated on every street corner. Cynthia and I became transfixed with getting to know one another. After leaving a folk music club, the five others departed for their respective hotels with a promise to meet at the Guggenheim the next morning. Energized by our discovery of one another, Cynthia and I headed off to the subway and to Coney Island. A cool Atlantic breeze muffled the sounds of the nearby Ferris Wheel and carried on it the smell of saltwater, the cries of gulls, and the chance for romance. We nestled into the warm sand and closed the gap between us with words. Except for an occasional beach-walking couple that would respectfully detour around us when they approached, we seemed alone on the island. When I told her I felt like I had known her forever, it was not a pick-up line. Our values and personalities were fraternal twins, character clones. Describing the night later to a friend, Cynthia said we had intercourse of the mind.

I told Wild Bill how Cynthia and I had spent most of the night together, hand-in-hand, walking the streets of New York, riding the subways, and talking about everything: ourselves and families, hopes and dreams, religion, architecture, Vietnam, politics and love. Outside the lobby of the Taft Hotel where she and her friends had a room, I planted my first kiss on her lips, a seed in both our hearts. "She is a dear friend," I concluded.

"Cool." No further comment from Wild Bill.

"That's it?" I protested. "I bare my soul and all you have to say is 'cool'?"

"Listen up now. I've got something to tell you. Ever notice how guys will take turns telling these elaborate fantasies of their future lives when they get back to the World?"

I answered 'yes' to grease the conversation, although Wild Bill was the only experienced Marine who ever took the time to talk to me.

"Right. Then you know how they describe every detail: The clothes they'll wear on a date, the cars they'll buy, every physical feature of their girls back home and how well they will make love; the moment-by-moment events that will make them gloriously content in that happy future. You dig?"

Again, I agreed, this time I realized he was also talking about me.

"They're fucked." His conclusion was part condemnation. "You live here, not in the World. This is your reality. Fantasy can get you killed. I've seen it."

He paused again but I urged him to go on.

"Three guys I knew played the fantasy game constantly. They didn't pay attention to Vietnam and then they paid for their mistake. A single Bouncing Betty took them out, one wounded and two KIA."

The Bouncing Betty land mine was an ingenious concoction made from unexploded ammo and trash, much of which had been left by U.S. soldiers. When triggered by foot pressure or a hidden trip wire, the Coke-sized mine sprang out of its buried position and detonated when it was groin height so the hot shrapnel could do the most damage.

I struggled with this lesson. Nothing gave me more pleasure than fantasizing about my girl back home, my Bridget. A perfumed letter from her and a simple "I love you" closing sent my spirits soaring. I carried the most recent letter with me at all times sealed with my wallet in a protective plastic baggie so I could repeatedly sniff the aroma of her words. My return letters gushed with romantic feelings for her. The lonelier I got, the more I needed her to be waiting for me. I moved to thoughts of her like the prisoner follows the isolated sunbeam that penetrates his cell. That hunger grew as the war wore me down. I wanted to keep Bridget unsullied by the ugliness of the war so I told her little. Eventually, the war shut me down emotionally and my letters to Bridget and my family dwindled to occasional desiccated paragraphs that merely informed of my being alive. It became easier to heed Wild Bill's wise advice.

During the first few months of my tour of duty, there was a lot of off-duty time at my fire support base. Relief for the troops came primarily from two drugs: Government-subsidized alcohol available at the Enlisted Men's Club, or marijuana joints available from the nearest Vietnamese supplier. The extensive use of drugs in Vietnam should come as a surprise to no one. Alcohol and other drugs are a time-honored response to the risks and boredom of soldiering.

A cultural divide formed around our escape of choice. Those who drank, the "juicers," partied separately from those who smoked, the "heads" or "dopers." My group, the heads, sought an inward and reflective refuge from the War that centered on small talk, stories, and total absorption in music. Music connected white America's Peter,

Paul and Mary with Motown's Marvin Gaye. Getting stoned together and playing music together helped the Brothers and the "Chucks," as we whites were called, bridge the racial gaps as we mauled songs by the Beatles, the Beach Boys and the Temptations on the cheap guitars purchased at the Post Exchange.

"Take a pause from the cause, man. You earned it," Wild Bill suggested as he passed me the number. Like every other day, the day I smoked my first marijuana cigarette included grueling training on the mortar interspersed with filling sandbags in three-digit temperatures. The danger of snipers, sappers, incoming B-40 rockets, and 82 mm mortars begat an undercurrent of anxiety. Mosquitoes, ants, spiders, and centipedes interrupted each night's sleep and swelled my eyes and face. Instead of skin, I developed a sunburnt hide with triple layers of bites. The mess hall food caused diarrhea so often I began eating only C-rats. Even without the danger, Vietnam rubbed the spirit raw. Grass was salve to the wound.

Just as I was learning to appreciate this smokable antidote to my perpetual exhaustion, our Platoon Leader raced out of the Fire Operations Center and screamed, **"Fire mission! Second Section, First Squad, get on your gun!"**

A spurt of adrenaline snapped open my eyes. "We're off duty," I said. Ignoring my lament, Wild Bill leapt into action. He jumped over the gun pit wall and then tore the poncho off the mortar.

Our squad leader, "Cowboy," dropped his barbells and raced to the primitive field phone in the gun pit where he took the mission parameters from the Fire Operations Center: "Listen up! One round, Willie Peter! Stand by to adjust for fire!" he yelled. I watched transfixed as our assistant gunner, "Vulture," ripped the packaging from the white phosphorus marking round. A few seconds later, Cowboy spat out the compass heading, elevation, and the number of gunpowder propellant bags to be left on the twenty-inch-long, green and silver shell. "Heading: Two niner zero. Elevation: forty-seven degrees. Leave four bags on. Repeat!"

Wild Bill set the targeting numbers on the gun sight while he simultaneously repeated them for Cowboy to confirm. He propelled himself in an artistic leap in the approximate direction of the target and pivoted the gun around its anchored base plate in the process. He had trained his bones to seek out compass headings. With a few tugs at the heavy bipod legs and deft cranking of the two fine-tuning wheels, he had the gun on target. Ten seconds had elapsed. Vulture pulled the safety pin on the round as Wild Bill rechecked his settings. Cowboy repeated the firing solution into the telephone.

Cowboy's order of "Fire!" was Wild Bill's signal to remove the delicate sight from the gun mount. Vulture tipped the round into the mouth of the tube and let it slide down the four feet to the firing pin at the base. Displaced air squeezed past the descending round and created a distinct hollow whistle. I focused on that sound—it resembled a base note from a large Andean flute.

"Fire in the hole!" cried Vulture. I quickly ducked and slapped my hands over my ears. The deafening blast and heat of the propellant charge arced over my back. Shards of sound echoed inside my skull like a camera flash in the dark reverberates inside the eyes. The round cleared the barrel and armed itself en route to some destination unknown to us.

"On the way," yelled Cowboy into the telephone. Less than a minute had passed since we had been cruising the galaxies on the near hallucinogenic properties of Nam marijuana.

We heard no sound of the impact. No sound of white phosphorus burning into whatever it touched.

Cowboy's next order broke a long period of stillness, "Three cranks up and one to the right. One round of Willie Peter!" Both of Wild Bill's hands flew on the adjusting wheels as if voice-activated by the order.

The squad's newest ammo humper, Crusher, yelled out "Got it!" He was a former high school football star and one of the few blacks on the 'smallsville,' Oklahoma team. His fullback shoulders rippled as he tore open the protective canister, ripped away the beeswax packaging, yanked the safety pin off the second white phosphorus round, and passed it with a lithe fluidity to Vulture who sent it immediately down the tube. "Whoosh. Kawhoomf!" The explosion of the propellant charge blasted away all competing sounds and left us in a crater of quiet.

Then, from Cowboy: "Fire for effect with ten rounds HE! I want High Explosive and I want it **now**! Let's rock and roll!" Vulture and Crusher prepped the rounds at lightening speed and Vulture dropped one after another down the tube. "Hey, cherry!" Cowboy screamed at me, "I said ten rounds HE. Get your ass in gear, you doper! Get with the program and I mean most ricki tik!" His harangue snapped me out of my trance and I joined the others in their efforts. In less than ten minutes, the mission was over.

Rather than wait for the results, Vulture and Crusher disappeared into the night and Cowboy resumed his weight lifting in front of the mirror in the hooch with his warm beer. Wild Bill and I slumped back into our prior positions lounging against the gun pit walls and I settled back down into the moment, trying not to think of home, Bridget, or Cynthia. Wild Bill was right back where he had been—stoned, relaxed, and apparently oblivious to what had transpired moments before. It was the first time I saw him perform. His speed and accuracy on the gun, I found out later, were unparalleled in platoon memory. I had observed an even more esoteric skill that night: His ability to go in a matter of seconds from stoned to stone sober and then back again.

6

Patrol: Quang Nam Province; May 1969

Since I was new to combat and ignorant of the actual ways of combat, I knew that I would not survive for long. I prepared to accept my death as well as I could. I clearly saw that it did not matter how proficient I was; a random rocket or mortar hit could end my life in an instant. This was not an abstract threat tomorrow or next week; it was thirteen months of 'now'—thirteen months of wondering if I would be alive to eat my next meal, to see the next sunrise or sunset. I began hoping that if I would surely die, I would get it over soon, rather than prolonging my suffering through the end of my tour.

—Daryl S. Paulson. Ph.D., *Walking the Point: Male Initiation and the Vietnam Experience*

"Drop your cocks and grab your socks! You're gonna walk the walk, First Squad!"

I pried open eyelids welded shut by too little sleep and the swellings of mosquito bites, to face wild eyes framed in black and green glaring down on me. "Get a move on, Marine! We've got a war to fight!" A musky scent ripe with sweat, fetid body oils, grease paint, and Lucky Strike breath fogged my head. I recognized T.J., the forward observer for our platoon, and his big crooked grin that blared through the camouflaged face paint. His bloodshot eyes slanted, almost Mongolian. Tethered to him and wearing a matching smirk that stretched full across a thin face was his ever-present side kick and radio operator, Long John.

Only half a bottle of Obesitol, the Vietnamese stimulant drink, could account for their enthusiasm considering they had spent the night in the bush calling in my squad's middle-of-the-night fire mission.

Cowboy turned away from the mirror he had set up in the hooch, lowered his barbells, and planted his hands firmly on his hips. His perfect tan accentuated his finely muscled physique. "Says who?" he demanded, head cocked slightly to one side.

"Yale," retorted T.J. We called our Platoon Leader, Cpl. John Swenson "Yale" because he attended two years of college there. "He wants the cherries to see the results of last night's mission, so saddle up your squad, Cowboy."

My first patrol. I shook my head awake, popped off my cot, and started shoveling things into my haversack—green sweat towel, C-rats, plastique explosives plus the blasting caps and hand generator needed to set them off, an extra pair of socks, an extra canteen, halizone tablets, mosquito repellent, and my entrenching tool. I trembled with an exhilarating nervousness. Excitement mixed with terror.

As I stuffed my flak jacket pockets with HE and concussion grenades, Wild Bill leaned over me smiling and combed the sides of his balding head with his fingers. "You don't need any of that shit. It'll just slow you down. A bandoleer for your 16 and a couple canteens will do just fine. Don't forget your first aid kit and get some cammy on your face and hands." I obeyed but kept the grenades for an extra measure of insurance. Within fifteen minutes, I was fully suited up and ready. Bedecked with body armor and rifle, I presented myself for Wild Bill's inspection and scowled for him behind the green and black war paint that hid my face. He tipped my helmet slightly to one side. "Cool," he pronounced.

About five hundred yards beyond the perimeter defenses of the fire support base, thick jungle foliage marked the edge of my known world. A small village on the edge of the jungle just south of the base hunkered amid rice paddies and some pitifully thin livestock, mostly water buffaloes. The villagers knew the rules: Anyone or anything outside the ville after dark was assumed to be VC.

"Move it out, jarheads, and be at the ready for anything!" T.J. ordered as he and Long John led Cowboy, Wild Bill, Crusher, Vulture, and me in that order out the base entrance and then south on the maintenance road that surrounded the outside of the base perimeter. Blinded by the intense morning sun, I dropped my head and tipped my heavy steel helmet forward for some inadequate shade.

"String it out. Don't bunch up," cried Cowboy. "Wild Bill, take up the rear and watch the FNGs," referring to Crusher and me. As Wild Bill faded back behind me to maintain the customary twenty-to-thirty-foot separation, Cowboy added, "Lock. And. Load!" Each word a sentence unto itself. I removed the first magazine from the bandoleer, tapped it three times on my helmet to seat the cartridges to the rear, and then snapped it into place just ahead of the trigger housing on my M16. With right thumb and forefinger, I pulled back on the cocking mechanism at the base of the combination handle-sight and let it fly. One round entered the chamber with the solid resonance of precision-milled metal seating itself home.

As Guard Tower Number 1 came into view, I wondered if anyone had told the guards we would be moseying through their fields of fire.

With characteristic bravura, Cowboy shouted an explanation to the guards: "Just out for a walk in the country." Then we came to Tower Number 2, the same tower from which I watched the slaughter of the two Vietnamese boys a few weeks earlier. I clicked my selector switch from "SAFE" to "SEMI" for semi-automatic fire.

As if he could sense my action, Cowboy called back over our heads, "Safeties on. I repeat: Safeties on!"

I complied and dropped my rifle from the awkward "present arms" position—rifle held diagonally in front of the chest—to a more relaxed position at my side. My right hand balanced it casually with thumb and forefinger around the narrow grooved cylinder between the magazine housing and the black plastic barrel grip. I wondered if the Colt manufacturers designed the little gap there just for this purpose.

The dirt road intercepted a narrow but well-worn path halfway between guard towers Number 2 and Number 3 where I had watched patrols head out and later return by this same route while on guard duty. Departing faces telegraphed angst; returning ones relief.

"Watch for mines. No cluster fucking, Marines. Keep a tight asshole and keep your distance," barked Cowboy, and he added sarcastically, "No more than one Marine per mine!" In spite of his 5'-6" height, blonde hair and baby face, he worked hard at living up to his nickname by adding an extra layer of machismo.

Tension grew as we approached the tree line, the wall that marked the extent of the tower guards' oversight and the threshold of the jungle. I stepped across that threshold and the jungle closed around me like the sea engulfs a diver. The filtered sunlight dimmed and took on a sickly yellow-green hue not unlike the odd glow that follows a summer thunderstorm.

Vulture stopped, turned, and whispered, "Silence. Pass it on." I turned but was further silenced by Wild Bill's knowing smile and nod. Grass and moss gradually replaced the sand and dirt on the trail. Further in, leaves, twigs, and small vines carpeted the path as it narrowed and snaked through the ever-thickening foliage. After a hundred yards or so, Vulture disappeared to the right. I snapped my M16 back to the present-arms position and concentrated my gaze. A small break in the living green wall revealed a narrow pathway with branches and vines dangling so low that it forced the gangly 6'-2" Vulture to make his way bent at the waist, his long neck craned forward.

I began practicing in earnest the Advanced Infantry Training skills I learned while stationed at Camp Geiger in North Carolina during the prior winter. For a couple of seconds, I opened my eyes wide and tried not to focus on anything in particular, "soft eyes" in Tai Chi. I trusted my peripheral vision to detect movement. Then I swept my eyes left and then right, always alternating my focus between close in and further out objects. As my view moved to the frontal position mid-sweep, I checked the exact route of Vulture now only ten feet ahead and scrutinized the ground before me. When he moved slightly left or right, I followed in his footprints. If his step tripped no mine, then that small piece of ground was sacred. An invisible lifeline connected us and our futures. Mines usually took out the triggering man and man behind. In like manner, Wild Bill's fate depended on my ability to spot danger.

Within half an hour, my head began to pound with a painful headache. I grew tired of the dank smell of the jungle and the salty taste of sweat trickling into my dry mouth. My eyes ached from scouring the landscape for tiny trip wires, for small disturbed mounds of earth and grass, for the glint of light off a metal barrel, and for the sound of language or movement other than our own.

I had trained for this. The six months of Stateside infantry training had a central focus on just this type of situation because it was the most dangerous we would likely face. I recalled war games the previous January while at Camp Geiger. On a night patrol in the North Carolina woods, I was point man for our training platoon. My orders were to lead my platoon to a predetermined destination any way I chose using my compass and map to pick the route through the forest. I checked my compass heading and led the platoon down a deer trail through a particularly dense area. After about an hour, the night exploded with a terrifying roar of automatic fire from only a dozen feet off to my left. What the blank rounds lacked in lead they made up in smoke and noise. I froze in fear and immediately realized another training platoon had executed a textbook ambush. I had led my platoon right into the trap. The ambush wounded only our egos. Then I discovered, to the delight of my training platoon, that I had wet my pants. Not just a little dampening; unwittingly, I had emptied my entire bladder.

No amount of training could be adequate for this, the real patrol, the real ambush, real punji stakes, and real wires set to trip Bouncing Bettys. There was far too much to know, to see, to hear, to smell. I needed the instincts of a hunter but had only the fear of the prey. Neither T.J. nor Cowboy gave us a word of briefing in preparation. If I die, I thought, I can blame them. Some consolation.

Mid-scan, I looked up. No Vulture. I whipped around to see Wild Bill. No Wild Bill. My heart pounded with the terror of facing this alone. I had lost my lifeline. I was abandoned and adrift. The ground ahead included no safe spaces to plant my boot. The tangle of trees, vines, and leaves closed in with a wet cloak of green, suffocating heat. I saw nothing ahead to indicate where five soldiers had just walked. Stunned, I froze in search of a clue and in search of the ambush I was sure awaited me. I knew the green shroud of vegetation would explode with hot lead at any moment. The enemy would wipe out our squad and either kill me or, worse yet, take me prisoner.

I wanted to cry out but my tongue glued itself to the roof of my mouth. With a lung's worth of air in a shouted whisper, I called out, "Vulture! Wild Bill!" Two firm taps on my helmet caused me to spin around and to discover Wild Bill's smiling face and pointing arm. I hurried in the direction he indicated and found Vulture climbing over the massive root of a tree. Perfect location for mines, I thought, but there were none.

I closed the distance to Vulture and soon found Cowboy and Crusher clustered around T.J. and Long John in an area where more light filtered through the jungle.

"Check it out," T.J. said.

At first, I noticed nothing unusual. Then Wild Bill walked toward a medium-sized tree trunk, a coconut palm with lightly mottled green bark. A little above eye level a jagged break exposed the fibrous guts. Missing were the trunk, branches, and leaves that formerly lived above the fracture. Seared shards of bark hung down from the soft marrow wood at its center like the molted skin of a snake. Something powerful had splintered the branches of the surrounding smaller trees and bushes and matted down the undergrowth. Flecks of metal caught the sallow sunlight and glinted lamely from surrounding tree trunks.

"Our mortars?" I wondered to myself.

"This is target number 9 from last night," explained T.J. "Wild Bill, remember this one, to the south at about 0200? You were the gunner weren't you?"

"That's an affirmative," Wild Bill replied through a wry smile. Although I, too, was on duty for the same mission, I did not remember when we had fired nor in what direction. High explosive rounds that exploded in rice paddies hardly made an impression. Mud and water absorbed most of the energy. In jungle areas, though, the HE and Willie Peter explosions felled trees, sparked fires, and flattened the underbrush where the round could penetrate the triple canopies of foliage. Explosions in dry, clear areas dug craters five feet across and two feet deep.

"Check it out," T.J. urged again.

"Over here!" called Cowboy. About fifteen feet from the amputated tree, a large fresh splinter some fifteen inches long and two inches in diameter protruded from the soil as if it were trying to send out roots and establish life once again. Its upturned end bore a jagged piece of shrapnel half the size of my hand. We took turns fingering the serrated edge and its dangerous sharpness. It felt warm as if it still carried some of the fire that shredded it.

"Check it out, Marines!" said T.J., this time more emphatically. This time pointing to something on the ground about a dozen yards ahead. He wore a rakish smirk on his face, hand on his K-Bar knife. Long John, always at his side with the radio, smiled broadly. T.J.'s fingers flew apart as he made the sound of an explosion and then pointed to the real reason he had brought us here. Parts. Body parts. He had targeted our guns accurately and we had kills.

I became feverish and dizzy from the intense, suffocating heat and the smell of rotting meat. My mouth dried to a sandpaper finish. Bile threatened to replace saliva. Flies buzzed in an excited frenzy over pieces of flesh, blackened by sticky blood. Flesh that only hours before held together live bodies of Vietnamese. The mournful wail of a howler monkey echoed from the treetops.

"Heavy shit, man! This looks like a face," Cowboy said, his voice a full octave higher, pinched thin in the surreal glow of discovery. As if an actor in a bad Western movie, he drew his .45 out and fired an imaginary bullet into the thing. "We really zapped those zipper-heads." I could see no face in the dark amorphous blob interlaced with stringy gray bands of sinew.

"No, it's intestine," said T.J., authoritatively.

The gnarled and disfigured tissue throbbed, resurrected with the help of thousands of maggots and flies. Crusher took two quick steps to the side and vomited. Cowboy shot him a smug sneer as Crusher wiped his mouth with his sleeve. T.J. then led us along the faint trail of oil-like blood through more areas of the jungle that bore the scars of our mortar blasts.

I did not want to see this. My body felt unbearably heavy as I forced it forward, knees wobbly. The mantra I had been trained to scream in boot camp on Parris Island went through my mind: **"Kill! Kill! Kill!"** This was a war of attrition. Grinding down the enemy's resolve one death at a time was more important than the control of terrain. This was the end we were risking our lives to achieve. Now the mantra had the hollow ring of a football cheer after a defeat. Now I saw the consequences of my actions. I stared at indistinguishable body parts, too aware of the fact that I had helped separate them from their once whole and human owners.

Agitation and anger grew inside me as the buzzing of the flies grew more intense, becoming like a drone of nagging voices—voices I had successfully ignored while a college student. Impassioned voices arguing either the value or insanity of the United States' involvement in the Vietnam War. I had lacked the determination and the courage to either wholeheartedly fight for or against this War. I turned deaf, adopting a course of passive non-decision, plugging along in youthful euphoria, letting my grades at Kent State University slip without thinking much about what would happen if I lost my college deferment. When it became obvious where my apathy was leading me, I hid behind concepts like patriotism, duty, and honor, concepts that burned off quickly in the War's crucible.

Again, Wild Bill brought me back, back to the moment. And, once again, Wild Bill made the moment fresh and real. "Don't worry about it, J. M. You'll get used to it."

His casual acceptance of the situation, his enlarging and warping of the bounds of normalcy to encompass this putrid scene, his non-judging sigh of relief that it was them and not him modeled a desensitized vision that focused only on self-preservation, that most tyrannical of instincts.

"Looking out for Number One," Wild Bill said. "There it is, man, there it fucking, sure as God-damn hell is."

Wild Bill was right. I did get used to it.

We retraced our steps to the base. Near the base entrance, T.J. spotted two coiled cobras sunning themselves against the sandbag wall of an abandoned guard post. They were magnificent, both easily seven feet long. By the time I reached them, they had reared up menacingly. Their hooded heads flared gold and red against their black shiny scales as they wove a ballet in the intense haze of late afternoon. We drew close and formed a semicircle around them. They were beautiful to watch, their dance slow and hypnotic. As if on cue, both opened their mouths wide to flash white fangs an inch in length. Cowboy opened up his M16 on full automatic. In a split second, cobra pieces splattered the wall. Naturally beautiful and dangerous though they were, we could not allow them to compete.

7

The People We Were Sent to Save from Communism: May 1969

Part of the love of war stems from it being an experience of great intensity; its lure is the fundamental human passion to witness, to see things, what the Bible calls the lust of the eye and the Marines in Vietnam called eye fucking. War stops time, intensifies experience to the point of a terrible ecstasy....War offers endless exotic experiences, enough "I couldn't fucking believe it"'s to last a lifetime.

—William Broyles, Jr. "Why Men Love War"

The Crush of War: Dogpatch

The piercing scream of the police whistle cut through the thick soup of dust and heat. Scores of people scurried to dodge the monstrous machines of war. The traffic cop was trying to bring order to the chaos at this intersection of Highway 1—Vietnam's coastal roadway—and a cross street near the city of Da Nang. His starched and pressed light green uniform, white arm band, gleaming white helmet, and, most surprisingly, spotless white gloves set him apart from the heat and filth of Vietnam and war. This was the distinguished uniform of South Vietnam's U.S.-supported National Police, disdainfully dismissed as the "White Mice." He blew his whistle again.

Were this a real city and not "Dogpatch," an artificial suburb created by the U.S. military on the outskirts of the true Da Nang City, people might have obeyed the whistle and halted. Were the people familiar with the rules of a city and not simple peasants driven by the War from their farms, they might have known what to do. The drivers of the numerous military trucks, pedicabs, bicycles, and "cyclos" might have remembered there were rules other than the one cardinal rule of war: survive.

Across the street from where I stood, an old woman, dressed in a tattered, dull white ao dai, threw up her arms and emitted a scream so shrill it replaced the impotent shriek of the police whistle. Her voice rose in cacophony with the nerve-jarring grate of metal being twisted and crushed. A Marine deuce-and-a-half truck that had been turning left directly toward me jerked to a stop before the upturned hands of the traffic cop. The truck's hood was higher than the cop's head. The truck's right side was somewhat higher than the left. A conical hat rolled on an arcing escape route toward me in the dust. Its wake led back to the gray head of an old man in black pajamas who lay on his right side still astride a downed bicycle that pointed toward the screaming woman on the far side of the street.

I took a step forward to gain a clear view and saw that the massive right front tire of the truck had rolled up on to the middle of the bike and the old man's spindly legs. The massive weight of the truck bore down, mixing bicycle parts with human leg parts. Next the traffic cop frantically motioned the driver forward. The driver complied, let off the brake and the truck completed the journey over metal and limb. A sound like the breaking of brittle chicken bones mixed with the taste of the dust.

Instead of crying out or crawling away, the old papa san eased down flat on his back in the street. His gray head and beard lolled in the slight breeze. I remember saying under my breath: "What an idiot! Didi mau! Move you dinky dao gook! Three feet and you'll be out of the truck's way." He did not move.

The traffic cop waved his hands authoritatively for the driver to stop again so the old man could escape or someone could help him. Instead, the truck kept coming; a leviathan that could be slowed but not stopped. A mournful groan wheezed from the old man's scrunched up mouth when the tandem tires on the second truck axle began their torturous climb up onto the rear wheel of the bicycle no doubt firing new shards of pain through the old man's broken legs. I saw his head turn to the left and stare at the giant tires on their course toward his bicycle seat and tiny midsection. He seemed to skip right by terror and slide into despair.

"Too late," I thought. "You're going to die, old fool. You should have gotten out of the way when you had the chance, dink."

For a second time, bike and bones lifted the truck. His head twisted back to the right and out spewed an agonized cry of pain that ended, all breath expended, in a gurgling sound from somewhere deep in his throat. The obstinate driver heeded the now frantic arm waving and whistle blowing of the traffic cop, and he jerked the truck to a stop in unison with a breathy groan that squeezed out of the old man. Then the truck lurched into reverse and backed off the bike's rear wheel. No more sound came from the crumpled mass in the black pajamas.

Two people materialized and grabbed the feeble, broken body and whisked him and the mangled bike back into the dust cloud on the other side of the street. They vanished in seconds.

The sound of the police whistle restarted normal time. The truck completed its turn through the intersection and the driver gunned the engine as he pulled past and enveloped me in a plume of diesel exhaust. The episode had slowed him down by less than a minute.

With a blithe indifference, I felt nothing except impatience for the old man. Then it hit me. Standing at that busy intersection, I sensed a hole where my values once were. I sensed a desiccated residue, like when a snake sheds its skin and leaves a dry husk of itself. It felt like the early stages of a disease that made the abnormal seem normal. War had infected me with a counterfeit conscience. I feared that later the disease and I would become one.

Mai Lee

I lived in their country for a year. I saw their nameless faces every day. Only one did I come to know just a little. Mai Lee offered me a small chance for redemption, a lifeline to my humanity. She was one of the many Vietnamese girls and young women who stood along the road-side and hawked warm pop, candy, cigarettes, and film to the soldiers as they passed in military vehicles. She was only thirteen. Many of the young women sold their bodies as well. "Marines number one, number one. Suckie, fuckie, five dolla." After what I have read about the Puritanical sexual morays of the typical Vietnamese Buddhist, only the most desperate of situations would have been sufficient to turn young girls to prostitution. If the girls learned to trust you, they would offer party packs, baggies containing ten joints rolled as plump as a non-filtered Pall Mall. One pack cost ten dollars in "Mickey Mouse Money" (Military Payment Certificates), but ten dollars American would buy you two.

Later in my tour, I frequently pulled assignments as security on ammo and supply runs so I became a natural to re-supply the heads in my platoon. Mai Lee became my supplier and I brought back a few party packs each trip. Several times I hopped off the truck for a brief visit with her and then hitched a ride on a later vehicle. I came to really like her freshness and innocence. Using the perverse logic of the war, I believed that I could save her from prostitution if I bought enough dope from her to help feed her family.

One night she invited me to dinner with her family. Little kids, several women of all ages, and one very old papa san busied themselves in the tiny hut made of scrap materials. I saw only one man of draft age but he was missing a leg. No one spoke to me, even as Mai Lee introduced me in Vietnamese to the adults. I towered over the diminutive Vietnamese but bowed in respect. They all kept a suspicious eye on me, especially an older women with shriveled lips that filled the gaps from missing teeth. Mai Lee and I sat on the dirt floor at a low table separate from the others and another woman served the meal starting with a bowl of pho, Vietnamese rice-noodle soup, and a small bowl of brown sticky rice. I skipped the rice, not aware that the Vietnamese respect every kernel as a symbol of life, God's gemstone, never to be wasted. I thought the main dish was a heavily spiced chicken stew but when I asked, Mai Lee pointed to one of the ubiquitous dogs running around the area. I felt uncomfortable so did not stay long, but smiled and bowed some more. Thereafter, whenever I made a purchase from Mai Lee, she would throw in a half pack for free. She was learning the principles of Capitalism quickly.

On my last visit with her, I told her I was leaving and admonished her to avoid prostitution and stick to business. She ran into her hut and presented me with a simple framed photograph of herself. The baleful look on her face is haunting.

8

Friendly Fire: Fire Support Base Puller; May 1969

The young dead soldiers do not speak. Nevertheless, they are heard in the still houses: who has not heard them? They say: We were young. We have died. Remember us....They say: Our deaths are not ours; they are yours; they will mean what you make them. They say: Whether our lives and our deaths were for peace and a new hope or for nothing we cannot say; it is you who must say this. They say: We leave you our deaths. Give them their meaning. We were young, they say. We have died. Remember us.

—Archibald MacLeish, "The Young Dead Soldiers"

Friendly fire: One of those euphemisms used to mask reality when soldiers injure and kill fellow soldiers. Innocuous words at first glance, but, on closer scrutiny, words that damn, words that shame. I carry that shame and guilt still, three decades after my friendly fire incident.

The two weeks before the incident were hell. My platoon and I spent that time on a major search and destroy mission south of Da

Nang. My entire mortar platoon had been in the thick of several fire-fights and had repeated fire missions in support of the rifle companies. During one two-day battle on May 12-13 that involved my platoon and several other Marine, Army, and ARVN units, we killed 292 enemy soldiers. It was terrifying, exhilarating, and exhausting.

After returning to the fire base, my First Squad had fire missions that kept us up half the night for two nights in a row. The next day, Wild Bill and my Squad Leader, Cowboy, rotated home. Before he left, Wild Bill gave me a bear hug and his extra pair of jungle boots. The boots wore out quickly but not his life lessons.

Cowboy's departure resulted in my getting his Squad Leader position in charge of the Second Section's First Squad and gun, and a promotion to Lance Corporal. I wondered if the promotion was a blessing or a curse as I gazed at my seriously under-manned squad. Chisholm was still quite green, having only recently returned to Vietnam after serving six months in the Navy brig in Japan for smoking grass while on guard duty. My other ammo humper, a kid fresh from boot camp named Vanderwert, was an innocent, near illiterate boy from Alabama who was built like a lumberjack. When he heard all our nicknames, he asked we call him by the one he earned at YMCA camp as a kid, "Bingo." We decided that wouldn't do so we called him "Dutch."

"Why not," Chisholm offered. "'Dutch' or 'Shithead,' either works fine." I knew to expect trouble from Chisholm.

My most trusted crewmember was a guy we called Speed. He was a former cook from Atlanta, who moved up from his assistant gunner position to replace me as gunner. His nickname played off the thick slow drawl of his Southern accent. He was slight and carried himself with a suave demeanor that exuded confidence. In time, his skill as a gunner would come to rival Wild Bill's.

The friendly fire incident happened at 0205 at the start of my second day as a Squad Leader. We had been firing harassment and interdiction (H & I) rounds at varying times all night long. T.J., our forward observer at the time, had picked out several targets from the prior day's patrols. He chose likely places the enemy might try to run supplies through—creek crossings, rice paddy dike intersections, hedgerows, and wooded hideaways. The idea was to deny the enemy safe haven within our tactical area of responsibility by dropping a few rounds of high explosives on these likely targets throughout the night.

Before he went out into the bush, T.J. and I had agreed on the sequence and timing for the night's targets. He had a vital stake in knowing his exact location and that of each target. He needed to be close enough to observe but still a safe distance beyond the ten-yard kill zone of our high explosive rounds.

The moist, stagnant heat of that night glued my utilities to my skin making it easier for a host of blood-sucking insects to feed. Their incessant drone lulled me. We all had learned to fall asleep in any position within a few minutes and then lurch to complete awareness within a split second as needed. H & Is reinforced this sleep/wake pattern. While my crew of five dozed, I fretted over my new responsibilities. I was in charge of our gun. My job was to target it. Lives depended on my accuracy.

The 81 mm mortar is a crew-served, indirect fire weapon; the largest carried by infantry. An expert crew can fire it a maximum of thirty rounds per minute for a maximum range of 3,650 meters—over two miles. It weighs in at an awkward 110 pounds, not counting the aiming stakes and their night lights, rounds, target plotting board, cleaning equipment, and targeting solution manual. The rounds range from seven to twenty pounds each plus the weight of their protective canisters. Any larger weapon was transported by machine, not soldier.

We knew our gun pit coordinates to eight digits, which means within a ten-yard-square box. I had before me the schedule of a dozen targets for the night and the coordinates for each. Firing solutions relied on calculating two factors: the compass heading from the gun to the target, and the distance to the target. Distance could be addressed in multiple ways. An ignition cartridge that resembled a shot-gun shell, located in the base of the round, provided the first stage of propulsion for the mortar round. The base area of the round had perforations and gunpowder bags attached around it. When the round was dropped down the mortar throat, it slid to the bottom where a firing pin activated the percussion cap at the end of the shot-gun shell. The explosive gases passed through the holes in the base of the round and ignited the gunpowder bags. The expanding gases propelled the round out the tube. The extreme acceleration triggered a weight-based lever that armed the round just after it passed beyond the barrel of the gun.

We used firing tables to figure the distance the round would travel at a given elevation and propellant charge. A large target plotting board that consisted of a clear plastic disk etched with a metric grid that corresponded with the eight-digit positioning codes gave us the distance and azimuth (compass heading) to the target. The firing solution matched the number of gunpowder propellant charges on the round and the elevation for a given distance. After charting the coordinates for the target and the forward observer, the disk could rotate to yield a direction and distance from the gun to the target. This gave geographic meaning when the forward observer would adjust fire with the order to move left or right, drop or add meters, or direct us to walk in the rounds along a tree line.

Every day on the fire support base included three or more hours of practice on the guns. All of us took great pride in our ever increasing skill levels. I learned to calculate a firing solution in under a minute. Within another half-dozen seconds, a good gunner could target the mortar to the right heading and set the elevation. The fluid precision of a mortar crew in action would please a gymnastics coach.

The first round was usually white phosphorus, Willie Peter. It exploded with intense heat and sent up a plume of white smoke the size of a house. Correcting instructions from the forward observer would typically bring the second Willie Peter round within 10 yards of the target. Since this was the kill zone of the high explosive round where ninety-five percent fatalities are predicted, it was close enough. Thus, we could hit a target within about ninety seconds of receiving the mission coordinates.

After each H & I mission, the gun crew removed the next mission's rounds from their individual cardboard cylinders and beeswax wrappers so they could fire the next mission and get back to sleep on or behind the sandbag walls of the gun pit.

Everything was routine as we fired the first two rounds on target number 11 at 0205 early that morning. Target 11 was located about two miles due north of our fire support base. Since our mortar platoon was stationed at the south end of the base, we fired over the rest of the base to hit the target. Few people knew that it was routine for high explosives and incendiary rounds to be fired through the night right over their heads. Round number three broke this routine. Instead of the solid blast of the propelling charge that sends the round to its intended target, I heard the characteristic "pop" that signaled a "short round." On a rare occasion, the gunpowder bags would not explode perfectly. With a weakened charge, the round would fall short. I knew by the soft sound that round number three would be very short.

I ran out of the Fire Operations Center bunker screaming "Check your fire! Check your fire!" just in time to hear the sound of seven pounds of high explosive and hot metal shrapnel rip open the night's silence. The round landed within the base. A siren followed a few seconds later. I strained to hear the dreaded cry, "Corpsman up!" Hundreds of heavily armed men scrambled to prearranged stations and scoured the night's blackness for the source of the attack. They were ready to launch a counter attack as soon as they were told the direction to the enemy. They did not know the source was from within.

I knew the procedure. Cease fire. Nobody was to touch the gun nor any of the remaining rounds until the inevitable investigation had been completed. My friend, Scrounger, the company's Ammo Corporal, was the first to arrive on the scene. He remained calm even as we both saw the medevac chopper arrive near the explosion. I did not know at the time how many had been hurt nor how badly. The smell of cordite hung in the air like incense for the Last Rites.

Consistent with the routine established for investigating incidents of friendly fire, Scrounger and I began the examination of the H & I schedule. There we discovered the second problem. According to the schedule T.J. and I had agreed upon, at the 0205 firing time, I was supposed to have moved on to the next target, target number 12. Instead, I had ordered the three rounds fired on target number 11. Unlike target number 11, target number 12 was to the south and thus did not require firing rounds over the base. Had I changed to target 12 as planned, the short round would have landed harmlessly just beyond our perimeter.

The realization hit me. The slogan that hung in the Parris Island mess hall came to mind: "To err is human, to forgive divine—neither of which is Marine Corps policy." Scrounger took charge immediately, rising to the demands of the occasion. He corrected the grease-penciled mission plan so it would show target number 11, not 12, for the 0205 firing. Then we learned about the casualties.

Scrounger was on the radio to the forward observer, T.J., cool as could be: "We had a short round inside of the base and we have casualties. I say again, we have casualties! Need to **confirm**, I say again, **confirm** the last H & I target and firing time." Scrounger slowly and deliberately read off the coordinate of the now amended target number 11 for the 0205 firing time. T.J. began to object, but Scrounger interrupted him and continued. "I say again. I will read the coordinate and firing time again and you will **confirm** them. Roger?" Then T.J. understood and confirmed the falsified target after Scrounger repeated it. Scrounger instructed him that there would be an investigation and that he must retain his copy of the target list and it must confirm the list from which he had just read.

Just as Scrounger signed off, an officer from Headquarters arrived to investigate the incident. He grilled each of us separately with dozens of questions and then concluded the cause of the friendly fire was the short round and that the target was a legitimate one. He filed no charges. The Base Commander issued a policy the next day prohibiting the firing of mortars over the base unless the base was under attack. He split our platoon in half and sent the First Section and its two guns to the north side of the base to cover targets in that direction. H & Is became more complex thereafter because two gun crews had to be on duty all night to hit targets all around the base.

Later that night, word was that the short round seriously injured three Marines. The next day we learned from the returning medevac chopper pilot that one had died.

The night of the short round incident, I walked out to the landing zone. The significance of the event crashed down on me. It was wartime and friendly fire was a daily hazard. What bothered me was that during the entire episode with the investigating officer, I thought only of myself. Like a mirror, the War reflected personal characteristics that I did not like. Shame brought tears, my first during my tour of duty. I pulled from my breast pocket the plastic baggie in which I kept Bridget's picture and latest letter with the hope of drawing comfort from the aroma of her perfumed stationary. Its incense held no powers of absolution. Instead, I wrote a confessional letter to Cynthia, my friend to whom I confided secrets, but I was too embarrassed to send it.

Scrounger tried to console me. "You had to fire over the base at other targets earlier that night, didn't you? Somebody could have grabbed that short round at that time with the same result." He was right. "When was the last time you had a full night's sleep?"

"Camp Pendleton, California" I replied.

"Were you smoking dope or drinking that night?"

I told him I never smoked or drank while on duty or while in the bush. "You know that, Scrounger, none of us do." Knowing it was an honest mistake was no relief. My mistake sent two men to the hospital and one to the grave while I scrambled to hide what I had done.

A few weeks later, Scrounger and I were shooting the shit in the Second Section's hooch when a rat the size of muskrat boldly scurried along the edge of the old ammo cases that formed the inside walls. I had been sharpening my bayonet and, with Zen-like aim from ten feet away, nailed his head to the wall with my blade.

"Scrounger," I said, "how's that for a one-in-a-million chance?"

"Yeah, one in a million. Just like your short round."

9

Dead Reckoning: Operation Pipestone Canyon, Go Noi Island Area; May 1969

The peculiarity of Red Army is that there is no fixed line of operations. The line of operations is determined by the directions of operations. No fixed directions, hence, no fixed line....Strike when you can win, and retreat when you cannot win. This is the most popular explanation of our mobile warfare....The enemy advances, we retreat; the enemy camps, we harass; the enemy tires, we attack; the enemy retreats, we pursue.

—Mao Tse-tung

The first quality of a soldier is constancy in enduring fatigue and hardship. Courage is only the second. Poverty, privation, and want are the school of the good soldier.

—Napoleon

Soon after I was promoted to Squad Leader and put in charge of First Squad's gun crew, Major General Ormand R. Simpson, Commanding

General of the 1st Marine Division, sent most of the Division on Operation Pipestone Canyon into the vicinity of Go Noi Island. The operation's objective was to rid the area of the 36th NVA Regiment, to clear it once and for all. However, all I knew at the time was that we were to search out, flush out, and wipe out the enemy. We hunted humans. I thought of it as another typical search and destroy mission, only much bigger and longer. Pipestone Canyon was considered the most significant 1st Marine Division operation in 1969. By the end of the month, we had killed more than a thousand of the enemy.

During the first days of the operation, we humped our tremendous loads through jungles, paddy muck, areas defoliated by chemicals, and elephant grass, but we had no fire missions. We were still carrying the original rounds but they were gaining weight somehow. Maybe they absorbed our heavy, dark moods.

I had one straggler in my squad, Pvt. Kevin Chisholm, the man who had come to my squad from the Navy's brig in Yakuska, Japan. I guessed that the ultra-regimented life of the high-security prison was the source for his smart-ass attitude. I didn't mind his unwillingness to pull his own weight. I didn't mind his disrespectful snipes. I didn't even mind his constant complaining. I did mind that he had dumped one of his rounds. Truth is, all that other stuff pissed me off as well, but dumping a round made me furious. I discovered this after a short break when I had let my squad walk by me so I could take up the rear position at the very end of the column. When I saw Chisholm had three instead of four rounds, I grabbed his pack to stop him and ask for an explanation. "It musta' just slipped outta my pack back there in the swamp," was his lame excuse. I explained the situation to Speed, my gunner, and told him to keep the squad with the rest of the mortar platoon while I marched Chisholm back to the place where the "slipping" was supposed to have happened.

I grabbed Chisholm by his lapels and shook him while I screamed into his face like my drill instructors had done to me. "What the fuck were you thinking, God dammit!? You know the slopes are going to use that round in their 82 mm mortars or make it into one hell of a booby trap."

"It just slipped out and I didn't notice it." He stared back at me with an expressionless face burnt crimson. Prison had prevented him from getting a protective tan before returning to Vietnam. Maybe it also prevented him from caring.

"Don't you bullshit me. You don't lose ten pounds of high explosives and not know it right away, you asshole!"

"I'm carrying over a hundred pounds—more than you. I didn't notice it." His deadpan expression remained unchanged.

"I oughta' write you up and have your ass sent back to the brig for this!"

"Fine. Write me up, then try proving me wrong."

My anger vented, the two of us retreated back along the trail until we came upon a swampy area. While he searched close to the path we took through the swamp, I took a wider swing in hip-deep water and muck near some mangrove-like trees. If I was to dump a round, that's where I'd do it. We both made discoveries. Chisholm found the round but I found two black, bloated bodies that had floated onto the edge of the swamp. The bodies, still recognizable as Vietnamese, were naked and swollen to where they resembled grotesque balloon floats with dolphin-like skin. The foul stench they bore also had a raunchy undertone of sweetness that surprised me. Hungry flies formed a second skin.

Chisholm made the dive for the round and we scrambled along the trail to rejoin the rest of the unit. It was not too difficult to return to the place where we had turned back for the round. Within five minutes of forward movement, we completely lost the trail in the tall grass and swampland. We tried to retrace our steps to find the point where we left the trail but instead got further turned around. I have a lousy sense of direction, and Chisholm's was no better. Back home before the war, getting lost just meant frustration, embarrassment, and delay. In Vietnam, it was life-threatening.

An intense sense of dread shrouded me. I could blame Chisholm for his laziness but it did not relieve me of my responsibilities for the both of us. In an attempt to return to the original heading, Chisholm and I tried to remember the relative direction of our shadows at the time we first turned back to retrieve the round. I drew a little map in the dirt with my bayonet and, based on the path of the sun, I projected where that shadow would be at the then-current time, which I estimated to be about two hours later.

I was isolated, unsure of myself, and terrified by the possibilities. I just knew that my every footstep was on top of a land mine. Every tree, every jungle bush camouflaged a VC waiting in ambush for me. My fears were well grounded. By 1966, the VC and NVA were nearly as well equipped, trained, and reinforced as the U.S. soldier. In addition, they had the advantage of logistical support, an elaborate tunnel net-work, and guidance from local village guerrillas through booby trapped areas. My head pounded with the repetitive phrase "We're lost, lost in a combat zone, and I'm responsible." The emotional bailing wire that held my wits together was near the snapping point. I began to fantasize about an ambush, a mine or, the mother of all fears, capture.

Then Chisholm started in with his whining, "What are we going to do? What if we're captured?" I wanted to shut him up with a quick butt stroke to the mouth, but did so with an order of silence instead.

We paused every twenty minutes for a few moments to listen. Fifty Marines on a daytime sweep is not a quiet affair. All I could hear was the constant, machine-gun-like banging of my own heartbeat. Then we heard a new sound—the whump, whump, whump of an approaching chopper. Chisholm turned toward the sound and began to jump up and down, and wave his arms in a desperate attempt to be seen above the tall elephant grass. My first thought was to jump for joy as well. Instead, I shouted **"Chisholm. Hit the deck and freeze!"**

I did the same. His Marine training worked this time and he did as ordered. I guessed that the chopper crew, spotting two armed men at a distance alone in the bush, might first assume them to be enemy not friendlies, especially if they did not signal with a colored smoke grenade—which we did not have. I did not want to take the risk of tangling with machine guns. I held my breath and began to quiver in fear as the chopper cruised almost directly over us at about one hundred feet in altitude and thirty miles an hour. I realized I was experiencing the same terror my enemies endured.

By early evening, after about five hours of humping alone, we noticed some distant voices. Vietnamese or English? I could not tell. Doing the low crawl, we crept up on the sounds until I saw a plume of smoke spewing from a hulking mass. Then the mass moved and I knew it was a tracked vehicle. We leapt to our feet and moved quickly to the unit of soldiers. They were an engineering battalion using forty-ton amtracs, Rome plows, and T-48 tanks to clear the jungle area of mines and cover. As if trained by the Catholic Church, we simultaneously dropped to one knee in reverential thanksgiving. We were alive. I enjoyed leaning over toward Chisholm and promising to ride his sorry ass when we got back to the base and give him all the shit duty for the next month.

10

A Terrible Beauty: Operation Durham Peak in the Que Son Mountains; July-August 1969

What does a man do? A man stands alone against impossible odds, meets the Apache chief in single combat to protect the manifest destiny of the wagon train, plays the guitar and gets the girl, leaps tall buildings in a single bound, plants the flag on Iwo Jima, falls on a grenade to save his foxhole buddies and then takes a bow to thundering applause. Death threatens only pets and grandparents. One thing is certain. Whatever it is that men do, they must leave home to do it.

—Mark Baker, *Nam.*

I remember the sounds of Operation Durham Peak. Flying over us nearly mile high, naval shells sounded like the flapping of pheasant wings. I remember the booming reports from the 105 mm howitzers on the base, the clang their big brass shell casings made when the gun crews ejected them into a scrap heap at their feet, and the heavy bang

74

of the breech as it chambered the next round. I remember the ear-split-
ting screech of the jets on their way to drop napalm, the scream from
our choppers on their way to drop us where the napalm had scorched
the earth, and the squeak from my gunner as he dropped into the fetal
position and hid in the dirt of the gun pit.

It was 0200, the time of night we all waited for, when cool night
breezes finally cut through the intense jungle heat enough to let us
sleep. But there would be no sleep tonight. Like the other members of
my mortar crew, I lay awake on my cot fully dressed, ready to go in an
instant to the landing zone where we'd load onto choppers that would
take us into the Que Son Mountains, into the battle we could hear in
the distance.

Some five miles east of us, the ships of the Seventh Fleet moored in
the South China Sea fired round after gigantic round at the enemy. The
soft slow whoosh of the shells disguised their murderous intensity.
The biggest shells were from the Battleship New Jersey, the flagship of
World War II fame. She boasted nine sixteen-inch guns that could
attack a target up to twenty-five miles away with shells that weighed
2,750 pounds each. After a few correcting rounds, her gun crews could
target an area as small as a single square yard and blow away an area
the size of a city block, assuming there was a city block that needed
demolition.

We were not used to the sound of naval shells or the welcome reassurance they provided. The enemy's 82 mm mortar rounds, rounds that
carried the sound of an isolated strong wind moving through trees as
they approached, were more familiar. So, too, was the sound of the
enemy's rocket propelled grenades. They roared in with a howl that
increased in volume and rose in pitch as they searched for their target—
as they searched for us. These were sounds of terror, not reassurance.

Speed, who lay on the bunk next to me, interrupted my meditation.
"I got a buddy on the New Jersey. He says firing a sixteen-inch round
is like throwing a VW bug across a big city." I could not shake the
image Speed planted, and I lay there picturing VWs full of explosives
soaring at the mountains to the west of us.

At 0430 the naval bombardment ceased and Marine artillery from our base and from nearby Hill 55 took over with their howitzers. Word came down to move it out. The brilliant muzzle flashes from the big guns served up surreal lighting as my mortar platoon slowly trudged from our two hooches toward the landing zone (LZ) to board the choppers. Light bounced among the low ominous cloud banks like lightning, blinding me to any familiar stars.

I placed my bulging eighty-pound pack on the metal floor of the landing zone and stretched out, using the pack as a backrest so I could better watch our artillery do its erratic dance to the cacophony of battle. This was more shelling than I had witnessed so far in my tour, and I shuddered to think of the strength of the enemy forces that must have been spotted to warrant such attention.

"Intelligence says we're gonna be up against the Third and the 21st NVA regiments," said T.J., who had joined me on the LZ. "They're tough sonsabitches." T.J.'s facial muscles twitched as he spoke, and he shifted his weight from one leg to the other. He was wired taut, and his nervousness added to my mounting apprehension.

The artillery crews ceased firing and T.J. hunkered down next to me as phase three of the attack began; Marine aviators now moved in to take over where the artillery had left off. We would be carrying out the final phase of the attack along with the 51st ARVN Regiment and ROK (Republic of Korea) Marines from South Korea. Although the scream of the planes flying at low altitude and near full throttle tore at my eardrums like a chain saw ripping steel, I was not eager to see them leave. When we took over, the enemy would finally have something to retaliate against. As we waited our inevitable turn in this deadly war game, more F-4B Phantoms, F-8E Crusaders, and A-4 Skyhawks released their deadly cargo of napalm and white phosphorus. Chemical fire, heat, and suffocation were effective means of flushing the enemy out into the open, making them more visible targets for the bombs and strafing runs that would follow.

At 0530 hours, our twenty-one-year-old Platoon Leader, Cpl. Swenson, finally got the order to board the nearby "Jolly Green

Giants"—the huge CH-46 Sea Knight helicopters. I hoisted my gear, M16, and mortar sight box and ran as best I could under the load. I led my five-man gun crew up the ramp and into the gaping maw of the chopper and took a seat near the rear.

As usual, it was hurry up and wait. Dawn was just beginning to reveal the fullness and darkness of the gunmetal blue clouds overhead. Morning light sharpened the senses. Eventually, the pilots powered up and the chopper strained. It seemed impossible for the beast to fly with the tremendous loads everyone carried, but the craft roared and rattled, and the jet engines screamed, and it did lift. After a few minutes, we were flying at over one hundred miles per hour and as smoothly as the TWA jet that brought me to Vietnam.

T.J. and Speed removed their helmets and climbed up the loading ramp to look down over its lip. I took the space between them. As I peered out, the sun broke over the horizon and splashed reds and oranges across the flat pewter undersides of the roiling thunderheads. Hurricane-force air pressure from the rotors washed my lungs of the base camp residues with fresh, cool air. The roar of the jets and the grinding metallic screech of the rotors prevented conversation. Spontaneously, the three of us screamed back at the roar and at each other. We flew down a line that separated life from death, and together we shouted our defiance. We shrieked for the simple thrill of being on the alive side of that line, fully alive to share one more sunrise, witnesses to the terrible beauty of war.

We were headed toward the low dark mountains and valleys about twenty-five kilometers northwest of Tam Ke—the place that had just endured five constant hours of high explosives and chemical fire. I wondered what we would find after landing. We climbed into the lush Que Son Mountains, great green thumbs that thrust up through the valley floors, veined throughout with streams. The beauty disguised the danger: Caves honeycombed the mountainsides. They were ready-made hideouts for the Viet Cong and North Vietnamese Army Regulars who waited patiently for opportunities to ambush. When they were ready to sneak out of these strongholds, I worried that the noise of rushing water would mute their movements.

We landed on a rocky shelf and raced out to the uncertainty beyond. The entire landscape was smoking. It seemed as though we had been deposited in an ancient time only a few billion years after Creation, when the Earth had not yet fully cooled. It was a terrible beauty. Everywhere were craters and parts of trees and shrubs, many still burning with the acrid, greasy gasoline smell of napalm. The chopper abandoned us. Its twin vortexes whipped the black smoke around into miniature tornadoes as it sped away.

At an altitude of thirty yards, the helicopter began to draw small arms fire seemingly from everywhere at once. The crew throttled the Jolly Green Giant up and almost right into the back of the mountainside in their efforts to flee the murderous gunfire. It escaped, leaving us to become the next targets.

I was awestruck. How could anything have survived our bombardment? We had pounded their mountain with all the modern weaponry available to the world's most powerful military short of nukes. They not only survived it, they waited until we foot soldiers arrived and then they pinned us down for thirty minutes with little more than small arms, rocket propelled grenades, and small mortars. Lying face down near a large rock with my hands protecting the back of my neck, I wondered what drove these people on in the face of such overwhelming firepower. My respect grew proportionately with my fear. They had to know that the bombardment was a prelude to our invasion force and that the scale of the bombardment was comparable to the scale of the forthcoming invasion. Later, when other Marines made disparaging comments about the VC and NVA, I remembered this moment. I remembered diving for the dirt and getting very small, indeed, because these Vietnamese decided we did not belong on their mountain.

Operation Durham Peak. The operation lasted for twenty-four days from July 20 to August 13, 1969. During the first two days in the Que Son Mountains, 255 NVA soldiers died along with 20 Marines from our First and Fifth Divisions, with another 100 Marines wounded. However, I knew nothing of this then. I only knew we were somewhere in the mountains southwest of Da Nang. I knew I was scared shitless and pissed off that I might die in this strange place fighting for something I neither understood nor cared about.

We could not continue hugging the Earth for very long or we would be dead. "Listen up, platoon! Get the guns up for direct fire!" commanded Cpl. Swenson. I ordered my crew over to a clearing twenty yards from where we had landed. It is amazing how fast a man can move in a squatting sprint while carrying two-thirds his own weight when the motivation is green tracer rounds sizzling overhead. My crew assembled the two-part base plate and stomped it into the unyielding ground as best they could without standing fully erect. They slipped the barrel through the heavy bipod and into the ball joint in the base plate. No need for the mortar sight for direct fire. Where would we fire? Everywhere I looked Marines were scurrying about, unloading choppers, digging in, and firing back with M16s, M60 machine guns, and M79 grenade launchers. If there ever was a prime time for some friendly fire casualties, this was it.

We were ready for orders, for a target. I was also quite content to stay flat on my stomach, thankful for the privilege of continued breath, although my lungs burned with the poison of white phosphorus and napalm fumes. Repeatedly, the Earth quaked again with the explosions of rocket propelled grenades and mortars around us, and we returned fire with a fusillade of our own that roughly retraced the trajectory of the incoming rockets. It was one of the few times during a fire fight that, because of a lack of a fire mission for the mortar, I had time to fire my M16 at the enemy. I emptied four magazines at the muzzle flashes that erupted from the nearby tree line to the east of our position. I have no idea if I hit anything other than rocks and trees. I do know that I wanted to. The thrill of staying alive while death threatens, and the thrill of causing death feel very much the same.

Corporal Swenson took a call on the radio from some invisible leader. With the receiver still at his ear, he barked the order "Prepare for indirect fire. Target coordinates will be ready most ASAP!"

Indirect fire meant we had to set out aiming stakes. Somebody had to venture some thirty yards out due north and due south to stick two five-foot poles into the rock-hard ground so that we could have something to aim at. I was very glad it was no longer my job. I had survived five months in Vietnam and had been promoted to squad leader. My ass was now much more valuable than Pvt. Chisholm's, to whom I gave the job.

We were ready when the mission coordinates came in. If the maps were so bad down in the flat paddy land, I wondered how they could be relied upon here in the mountains. I tried to recall the adjustments needed to fire on a target that is at a different elevation than the gun. The target was in a tree line located about four hundred yards away on a slope across the valley that lay to our northeast. Since it was at a higher elevation, I compensated by decreasing the range calculation slightly.

In a minute, I had the firing solution and I shouted it to my gunner, Speed, who laid the gun on target. Seconds after we fired a Willie Peter round to mark with smoke, a milk-white cloud mushroomed silently out of the rocky mountainside. Red comets trailing white tails arced away from the core of the thunderhead we had unleashed. Seconds later, the muffled boom of the explosion rolled across the valley floor to us. The platoon's forward observer called in adjustments to the coordinates and directed us to fire for effect with three rounds of high explosives. Against the dark rock and sky, the first HE flashed a brilliant yellow-red and spewed a volcanic projection of rocks, dirt, and whole trees. Like thunder, the explosion echoed around the battle zone over the din of small arms fire and the enemy's 40 mm rockets. Then the other three 81s from our mortar platoon opened on targets of their own. Surprisingly, things quieted down in a hurry. The NVA retreated to fight another day.

Having secured the LZ, we got orders to move over to another mountain top. Just a slight fuck-up, we were told. Apparently, that was where we were supposed to have landed. I wanted to just sit still, to remain where we had survived the counter-attack. It seemed safer, but somebody said we must move, so we moved. We balanced our loads, now lightened by four rounds, and headed over the rough terrain for the rest of the day. Although the mountain top was within view about eight klicks away, it was an all-day hump to get there. Sometimes the climbs were so steep we had to pass the packs and parts of the gun first and then use rifles and slings to haul the next person up. Fortunately, we all had lost weight due to the bad food and heat. By that time, I had slimmed from my normal 155 pounds to a bantam-weight of 120 pounds. The day's routine was to hump for about an hour and take a fifteen-minute break. I had mastered the art of sitting down propped against my pack and falling into a deep sleep in seconds, a useful skill I employ to this day. Those rests were precious.

The mountains were very different than the tangled jungles thousands of feet below at base camp. The air had cleared and now tasted pure and cool. There were deciduous over-story trees with little underbrush. We drank with abandon from the pure mountain streams, not even bothering to add halizone. Long views, no bugs; it was such a contrast to the jungles and paddies where the land and its inhabitants gnawed you down.

By early evening we reached our new position and could look back at our old LZ. It looked so close yet it had taken us all day to go the extra eight thousand yards the chopper crew had miscalculated, a distance they could have covered in about two minutes.

Cpl. Swenson told us that one or more companies of NVA Regulars were expected to attack within the next few days. We were positioned to serve in a blocking role to deflect them toward positions that were manned by Army units to our east. Of course, we could always end up being receivers instead of the blockers.

The other three squads built gun positions while Charley Company's grunts dug in as perimeter guards, Cpl. Swenson sheilded his eyes from the setting sun and pointed towards a small plateau of rock and dirt about three hundred yards to the east. "J.M., I want your squad to set up over there." It was lower, more exposed than the main area and had a more commanding view down the deep "V" of the valley to the north. "If the NVA are going to pay us a visit, I want you guys to be the first to greet them."

I led my five men across a saddle to the isolated outpost. We set up the gun, built low walls of sandbags around it, and dug our foxholes as best we could in the hard-pack, forming a small hexagon with a fifty-yard radius around the gun. I went over the fields of fire for all of the positions, assigned the watches for the night, and reminded my crew to use grenades if they heard or saw anything. A tossed grenade offers no muzzle flash to give away your position. In the dwindling light, we opened our gourmet C-rat meals with the handy little P-38 can openers and cooked with heat tabs and C-4 plastique. I went over in my mind the rules for a guard position and wondered if I should assign a password. It was an absurd thought, considering no Vietnamese could approximate English any better than we could Vietnamese. Any cursory question-and-answer exchange would easily distinguish an enemy soldier from a Marine. I just wanted an edge, any edge.

I stole a final look at Bridget's picture as the sunset extinguished my most important sense. Countless stars riveted a black dome to the sky. Hundreds of men desperately tried to pierce the night's opaqueness for an early warning of the expected enemy. I stared so hard into the dark I had to reach up and touch my eyes to make sure they were open. It was like trying to see the dark side of the moon. I felt completely alone and inconsequential.

Suddenly, a grenade explosion grabbed my attention. One hole over Dutch had heard something, then had seen something, then tried to blow something up. Not only were we now completely alert, so was everyone else on that mountain, enemies included. I sensed nothing. We were maintaining radio silence, so no one called to see what the hell was going on.

A few hours later on my watch, I saw something move about twenty yards out from my position. A moment later I heard a rustle and saw a shape move in the inky blackness. The stars were poor illuminators. I knew that if I looked long enough and hard enough, I would see what I was looking for, whether or not anything was there. I opened my mouth to quiet the noise of my breath and saw it a third time. This time I pulled the pin on an M26 fragmentation grenade but paused. "Identify yourself!" I ordered. Hearing no response, I threw the grenade at the phantom and shouted, "Fire in the hole!" toward Dutch's foxhole and took cover from the small blast. It must have worked. I saw and heard nothing the rest of the night.

When the sun rose, we broke down the gun and saddled up for the short hike back up to the main group. "You people a little jumpy last night?" asked Cpl. Swenson with a detectable grin.

When the orders came a few hours later to hump out of the mountains, we all wished we had fired more rounds on that bleak shelf the day before so our loads would be lighter. Our long column of about two hundred men bunched up. We were not keeping enough distance between each of us to avoid multiple injuries if one of us tripped a mine. The cause of our bunching up was an engineering company's efforts to blow in place several unexploded shells. I posed some of the engineers for a photo with a twelve-inch naval artillery shell that was easily four feet high. As we left that area, I heard the warning in the distance from the engineers "Fire in the hole!" several seconds before the huge blast. Next was that sound again, the whistling whisper, but this time it increased in pitch and volume as it got nearer. I froze in my tracks, not sure which way to dive. A piece of shrapnel the size of a fender from a '69 Buick buried itself with a loud thump and a sizzle into the dirt less than two feet in front of me. One step more and I would have been a foot shorter due to "friendly fire."

As we descended the mountain valley, the heat began to build. Each step took us closer to the heart of the furnace as the sun rose in the clear sky. The humidity staggered us. It was like breathing dirty gauze. After humping all day with seventy to eighty pounds of gear and armaments, we finally arrived as the sun set at our destination, a U.S. Army fire base. The Army was to be our gracious hosts until choppers could be freed to ferry us to another area where we would continue our search-and-destroy mission. Rivalry between the branches of the U.S. military runs deep, and so I did not expect to be given first-class accommodations. Judging by the result, I imagined a conversation between the commanding officers of the two service branches to go something like this:

Army officer: "Welcome to my base. Where would you like to bivouac your men?"

Marine officer: "We're Marines. Put us in the most inhospitable place available."

They did. We were directed to drop our gear in a completely barren area covered deep in sand close to the LZ, our departure point. To express our deep appreciation, we spent the remaining four hours of daylight building four low-walled gun pits that the Army could use after we left. I spent more time filling sandbags than anything else during my tour of duty. I became so accustomed to this mindless activity that to commemorate it, I painted on my seabag the inscription "On the seventh day God rested—and Marines filled sandbags."

The night was uneventful. With no guard duty to pull, we all slept soundly. As the heat of the next day began to build, I realized the problem we faced. We were sitting in a frying pan. Looking across the dark metal plates of the LZ, the horizon danced and shimmered. Each Army chopper that came and went churned the sand into dervishes that ground into our every orifice. We rigged makeshift shelters by stretching our poncho liners out from the gun pit walls and using our rifles as tent poles. The heat was as unrelenting as the boredom. Fortunately, there was plenty of clean water. We didn't have to add two or three halizone tabs to kill off bugs and strain it with our teeth when we drank.

Finally, night came again and with it, wonderful cool breezes. We were not to have two peaceful nights in a row, however. Sometime in the middle of the night, the first rocket propelled grenades roared into the main part of the fire base followed by heavy mortars. The base siren wailed and the warning of "Gooks in the wire!" blared over the loudspeaker system. Several fires blazed brightly. Green tracers began to criss-cross at eye level from the east and southeast. Our yellow and red tracers marked the return fire from dozens of locations. We were in the middle of a fireworks show.

Immediately, we were on the guns. Since Army patrols were outside the perimeter engaging the attacking forces in close combat, HE would have posed too great a risk of friendly kills. Instead, we were to place illumination rounds above the enemy troops to the east and southeast. Since this was to be direct fire, I did not have to develop a precise firing solution for a distant target. For this kind of mission, I knew the firing solutions by heart. That freed me to take over the gunner position. It also bumped my gunner, Speed, to the assistant gunner position for the battle. This was the riskiest job of all because the A-gunner was responsible for dropping the rounds down the tube. The A-gunner had to stand up to do the job.

The illumination round, at about thirty inches long and over ten pounds heavy, was the largest one we carried. Each round had an adjustable dial in the nose cone to allow the internal fuse to burn long enough so that it would ignite the white phosphorus inside just after the round would reach the maximum point of its arc. A parachute would slow its descent during its one minute of burn time.

Speed rose not one centimeter higher than needed to tip the long white round into the mouth of the tube. The nearly vertical mortar tube required him to stand almost upright, exposing everything above the gun pit walls to enemy fire. For Speed, that meant his crotch and all points north. Once the round was in, he beat its descent to the ground. I guessed he feared making a widow of the beautiful wife he bragged about so much. Our prominent muzzle flash drew fire. Our position was isolated near the southern end of the base and very close to the battle between Army patrols and NVA just beyond the perimeter. Perhaps NVA probes had determined that this was a weak part of the perimeter. It had juicy aircraft targets on the LZ.

Rocket propelled grenades were coming in thicker now, combined with mortars and deadly rifle fire. An 82 mm mortar round exploded so close to us that the shock wave ripped off Speed's helmet as he was diving for cover. The blast continued to drum around the inside of my head. Bullets and shrapnel zinged by and cut into our makeshift bunker walls. I overheard Speed complain that we should have built them higher. As our illumination rounds drifted down, they cast an eerie pallor over the entire scene and created multiple silhouettes that danced and lengthened as the flares lolled on the breezes. Depth perception was not to be trusted in this eerie light. This was an otherworldly glow that created as much illusion as it revealed reality.

Once again, Speed nervously began to get up from his prone position to bring the next heavy illumination round up to the mouth of the gun. I backed off the elevation of the gun a half turn to compensate for the settling of the base plate. A iridescent green tracer round from an enemy machine gun and two tracking bullets popped close by Speed and thumped into the inside of the far wall of the bunker. I wondered what a bullet to the gut felt like while three rivulets of sand bled from the sand bags. Speed's eyes lit up wide as saucers, he let out a piteous little whine and let go of the round as he dove for the nearest bunker wall. The round landed square on the vertebra of my neck, knocked off my helmet, and cracked onto my head. Whatever pain followed only fueled the heightened thrill of the firefight. Instead of feeling anger at the quaking man cowering paralyzed with terror in the corner of the pit, I only felt disgust. With eyes peering out from under the lip of his helmet and one hand clutching his nuts while the other repeated the sign of the cross, Speed made himself as small as possible. He shriveled inside himself and was not about to come out. Since this was direct fire, I did not have firing solutions to plot. I was free to take over his job, too. It was a convenient rebuke aimed at Speed.

It was exhilarating, wonderful. I let out a war whoop each time I boldly stood fully erect to drop another round. I was fearless, invulnerable, and incredibly alive. I knew the job was dangerous, but, like drugs, I relished the fix.

The firefight lasted forty-five minutes and then tapered off. Army patrols returned to the base and GIs shredded the countryside with beehive rounds from their 106 mm recoilless rifles, each round with eighty-five hundred flechettes that were an inch long and shaped like miniature darts.

After the battle, an eerie emptiness crawled out of the jungle. Later, as we relaxed over a cup of hot chocolate, I got up to refill my canteen cup and blacked out. When I came to, I was looking up out of a grave at the concerned faces of my squad. Little light-worms squirmed before my eyes like the birds for an unconscious cartoon character. I wondered if I had died. It took two of them to pull my limp body out of the foxhole into which I had collapsed headfirst.

Marine choppers came the next morning and ferried us to another area for another ten days of humping the bush. When we finally returned to our base, Cpl. Swenson informed me that the Base Commander had heard what had happened on the Army fire base and recommended me for a battlefield promotion to corporal. With the promotion came another stripe and an extra $30 a month to add to my $105 monthly salary. That thirty-five percent pay raise is still the largest in my life.

11

The End Justifies the Marines: Dodge City; September 1969

For all of the glory words like duty, honor and valor, war runs best on evil, a breeder reactor that vomits out a hell full of pain for the little spark of sadism people feed into it. Evil was encouraged with rewards of medals, time off from the horror, a hot meal. How else can you convince boys to kill one another day after day? And when the darker side grabs the upper hand, takes control, how else can it be excused?

Vietnam veterans do not have the luxury of dismissing evil as a momentary aberration in an otherwise civilized world. They have seen the ugliness humans are capable of inflicting—that they themselves are capable of inflicting.

—Mark Baker, *Nam*

Numerous studies have concluded that men in combat are usually motivated to fight not by ideology or hate or fear, but by group pressures and processes involving (1) regard for their comrades, (2) respect for their leaders, (3) concern for their own reputation with both, and (4) an urge to contribute to the success of the group.

—Lt. Col. Dave Grossman, *On Killing: The Psychological Cost of Learning to Kill in War and Society*

When my Second Section was on a mission together with Charley Company's Third Platoon, a rifle company, we had a contract. Charley Company encircled us at night and we provided them fire support whenever they went on forays to flush out the enemy. We were all under the constant threat of snipers, incoming rockets, and mortar attacks, but we were a support unit. They walked the point. They served as bait. They enticed the enemy into a fight, ambushed them if possible, and tried to kill them without being killed. The riflemen of Charley Company had the "thousand-yard stare." Aged well beyond their years, their eyes had an unfocused, vacuous quality. They did not look **at**, they looked beyond. They wore their stares as a badge of honor and a warning sign to keep a distance. They had seen and caused too much brutality at too early an age to completely digest the poison of it all. I learned to look at them slightly askance with the same non-threatening, peripheral view park rangers advise you adopt if you surprise a grizzly bear.

Ground fog hovered low over the black, interlocking steel plates of the base's landing zone (LZ) and dampened our spirits as we prepared for our joint search-and-destroy mission. The thirty or so Marines of Charley Company's Third Platoon and their corduroy-faced Company Commander, Lieutenant Smith, clustered close to one another on the LZ. Their prior search-and-destroy missions and the resultant losses of many comrades from mines and firefights with the NVA and VC had a solidifying effect. They were a tight unit.

I saw in each steeled face the fear and the thrill of the pending mission. I saw a determination to survive but also a sense of accountability to comrades on the battlefield. The fear of inadequacy was more basic than the fear of death—the fear that one's lack of skill, bravery, toughness, or even good luck would result in harm to the unit. It is better to be killed by the booby trap than to have carelessly triggered the trip wire that instead kills your buddy.

We anxiously awaited helicopters to airlift us to our destination, a rice-growing area between the Vu Gia and Thu Bon rivers northwest of An Hoa, better known to us as Dodge City in the Arizona Territory.

The American code names for these places conveyed images of cowboys and the Wild West. Appropriate, since the Arizona Territory had a bad reputation for lots of enemy activity. Periodically, from their mountain strongholds in the west, the NVA launched raids on the villages, stole grain stores, and drafted boys and men at gun point.

What I witnessed and participated in were efforts to clean out areas dominated by the NVA and the VC by destroying villages, defoliating crops and jungles, and relocating peasants to more secure locations. I knew nothing then of the Vietnamese way of life nor its unique religious and cultural blends of Confucianism, Taoism, and Buddhism. Consistent with religious and cultural tradition, Vietnamese farmers fertilize the fields with the family's food, bodily wastes, and the bodies of their dead. Our "pacification" and forced relocation programs severed their spiritual and biological lifelines to their ancestors. I saw little evidence to support the common notion that the politicians tied the hands of the military. Halfway through President Nixon's administration, the United States had dropped more explosive tonnage on Indochina than it had in both the European and Pacific theaters during World War II. Those of us fighting on the ground in 1969 were the targets of the enemy's anger and resentment that rose against the American strategy.

Instead of cultural awareness, combat soldiers, especially Marine grunts, valued grit, ruthlessness, and survival. I was no exception. The typical rifle company grunt spent two or three weeks humping a heavy load all day long in the bush. He'd serve half the night on guard duty, getting by on snatches of nightmare-laced sleep, and coping with everything the country could throw at him: exhausting climate, fire fights, snipers, mines, ambushes, the death of close buddies, and the struggle to determine whether the Vietnamese he encountered were friend or foe. After a stint in the bush he would get a day or two off at a fire support base to sleep and escape for a time with the help of marijuana, alcohol, or whatever else he could get his hands on. Then he would start a routine of night guard duty and patrols near the base. A few weeks later the cycle would repeat. If he was still alive at the halfway point of his tour of duty, he started a zealous tally of the days and hours calculated to the moment when he could return home to the States. In the meantime, we were all trying to be heroes in each other's eyes, or at least not cowards. We all craved graduation from the war's initiation rites of blood, cruelty, and random violence, and admittance to the elite club of hardened combat-tested Marines. Marines with the thousand-yard stare.

While Charley Company's Third Platoon huddled nearby on the LZ, my Second Section made final arrangements to serve as their mortar support. The sun fired its first rays over the horizon, melted the fog, and signaled its intent to do the same to us later. Manning the Section's two guns were two squads of five men each, half the complement called for in the Marine Corps operations manual for the 81 mm mortar. The manual also called for a commissioned officer—a lieutenant or captain with years of training and a college education—to serve in the Section Leader position. Fine in theory, but attrition due to casualties and rotation lead to Vietnam being termed the "corporal's war."

Our Section Leader at that time, T.J., had achieved a high school diploma and the rank of corporal. Neither of the Section's two Squad Leaders were sergeants (E-5) or higher as called for in the manual. Vulture and I were Lance Corporals (E-3) with less than four months' experience as squad leaders.

As we waited for the arrival of the choppers to air-lift us to the drop-off zone, T.J. readied our unit with calm assuredness. He stood in the center of our group and rattled off a memorized checklist of equipment.

"Vulture, J. M., are your squads ready? Gun sites secure? Plotting board and firing tables? Aiming stakes and lights? Four days' C-rations? Are you Marines ready to kick some ass?"

Vulture and I reported in the affirmative. T.J. checked each member of the unit in sequence according to the pieces of the disassembled gun they carried—mortar tube, bipod, inner ring of the base plate, outer ring. He inventoried the type and number of rounds. Being severely undermanned, we could only carry thirty-three. He shook each man's back pack to make sure the equipment and rounds would not fall out when we disembarked from the chopper and ran into the bush for cover.

"Good," he proclaimed with a confidence-building slap on each man's helmet.

The last man T.J. inspected was the newest to the unit, Dutch. "Check out my new lighter, sir," Dutch offered with a friendly tone. T.J. fingered the shiny new Zippo and its weighty metal medallion of the Marine Corps symbol emblazoned on one side. Turning it over and raising it to eye level to catch some sunlight, T.J. read the fresh inscription on the back with a prayerful voice.

"When I fall, to St. Peter I will tell: Another Marine reporting, Sir. I've served my time in hell." It served as our invocation.

After a radio check on the heavy PRC-36 radio, T.J. retired a few yards away from the rest of us to review alone the mission plan and map for the Arizona Territory. Before T.J. took command as our Section Leader, he had earned my respect as the section's forward observer. In a mortar platoon, the forward observer and his radio operator had the most dangerous, the most essential, and the most difficult jobs. They were gods who tempted the Fates. Like tunnel rats, first lieutenants, and helicopter door gunners, their average life spans in Vietnam were short. Armed with an M16 rifle, binoculars, maps, compass, radio and three-to-five days' rations, T.J. and Long John, his radioman, would scour the hinterlands for enemy targets. The thought terrified me. They had to know where they were at all times, anticipate where the enemy would be, avoid mines and ambushes, and then call in fire missions. If they miscalculated their position, they could easily target themselves. I knew the task would have been impossible for me. I rarely knew where I was, I was terrified of mines and ambushes, and I really wasn't gung ho enough to take on additional risks for the South Vietnamese government.

The tough back streets of blue-collar Pittsburgh had incubated T.J.'s unsettling intensity. He thrived on a reputation of being a little on edge, unpredictable, his hand on his ever-present 8-inch K-Bar knife. He had survived the tests of battle so far without crumbling. Being an infantryman suited him. No longer an initiate in the War's rite of passage, he was a full-fledged combat veteran with a penetratingly hollow thousand-yard stare.

Twenty years old and invincible, he loved to test his mettle. A couple of beers and a few tokes and he was ready to insult someone for being "plastic." I recall the night he and Long John returned from three days in the bush in a futile search for targets for our guns. That night T.J. chose as the object of his venting our Platoon Leader, Corporal Swenson, whom we nicknamed "Yale" because of his claim to have attended that university for two years before enlisting in the Marines. He said he joined up out of a sense of national duty, but nobody bought either claim—except me. I had the same situation, different school.

"Plastic," T.J. proclaimed as he walked about the Second Section's hooch that night. "Yale's a plastic bastard," he pronounced with a steel-hardened cynicism for the benefit of the four of us who were relaxing in the hooch. "He can't handle this shit. He don't know what the fuck we're about here." His pugnacious face took on a blood-red hue that even overpowered his perpetual five-o'clock shadow. Both hands shaped into pistols that poked toward the floor. "If you ain't with the program, I don't care how smart you think you are or how much a 'bad ass' you pretend to be, I guarantee, you're the fucker that's gonna' get us all killed." As he paced the full length of his anger, veins throbbed on his forehead like acid through a hose, a road map of his emotions. "Plastic melts and plastic breaks" he raved on, "and plastic people cry 'cause their bitch back home's doin' some other dude instead of waitin' for 'em. And they miss their mama 'cause they're scared." He spit out through the door flap of the tent as he left us with closing words, "Shit! Didn't they learn in boot camp like the rest of us 'being a man and being a Marine means you never give up?'"

Several times, I saw him use this aggressive approach to provoke a tension-relieving fist fight with anybody willing to take him on. I never saw him back down or lose a fight. After one fight, I watched him cock his head to one side and squeeze a grunted laugh through gritted teeth. Spit and blood drooled out one side of a sardonic grin. He didn't care. "I love this fucking place!" he boasted.

I staked my life on his primitive clarity of purpose and envied his self-confidence as I anxiously awaited our departure from the LZ. Finally, from the direction of the rising sun, two CH-46 Sea Knight choppers arrived, flying in from the Marine Air Station at Marble Mountain. I rose, shielded my face from the prop wash with my helmet, and lost my balance when my eighty-pound pack nearly toppled me over. Even before touch-down, Charley Company's Lt. Smith ordered his men to scramble aboard both helicopters. Within seconds they lifted off filled to capacity, leaving us choking in their dust.

"Not to worry," T.J. told us in an even voice. "We'll catch up to them." About an hour later, the third chopper arrived to take the twelve of us deep into the Arizona Territory.

We flew in low and fast at well over a hundred miles an hour. We were so close to the trees and rice paddies they looked like a green fur through the craft's circular windows. After a smooth, twenty-minute ride, we slowed abruptly and descended into a clearing where the grass was already beaten down. Before the wheels and the rear ramp could touch ground, most of us had already hopped out and followed T.J. into a thicket of trees. The chopper lifted immediately and sped away to safety. After quick consult of his compass, T.J. lead us into the triple-canopy jungle.

Seven-foot high elephant grass sliced at any exposed skin and slowed our progress toward our rendezvous point. Three exhausting hours later, we picked up the trail left by Charley Company's Third Platoon and took a well-deserved break. I did a right-face, peed a dehydrated stream of orange juice against the stalks of bamboo that flanked the trail, and collapsed. Within the perfect shade of the umbrella branches of a nipa palm, my eyes captured the halting movements of a tiny red, green, and tan gecko that clung to a stalk of bamboo five feet from me. The last thing I recall before sinking into a deep sleep was the sensation of sweat pellets that burned their way out of every pore and signaled mess call for all flying and crawling insects. Twenty minutes later, I awoke to an acrid smell that stole in on the wings of flies. It engulfed me, stung my eyes and nostrils, and almost made me retch. I caught my breath to halt its contamination of my lungs.

"Saddle up, Second Section," T.J. ordered. "Saddle up and move out now!" Within minutes, we came upon a clearing in the jungle. Tidy rice fields encircled a small village. Black smoke billowed above the high protective living hedge of bamboo that ringed the village and screened it from view. The entire area was supposed to have been cleared of friendly Vietnamese prior to its designation as a free-fire zone. All remaining life was considered VC. If it was dead, it was even better VC.

The thick vegetation had sheltered the village from aerial view, bombardment, and dioxin-contaminated Agent Orange defoliant, but it could not protect it from Charlie Company's Third Platoon. The grunts had burned it to the ground. Scattered around were broken fences, spilled stores of grain, and dead livestock. We remained in our single-file procession, silently alert for warning signs of reprisals. Only the devouring buzz of flying insects and the sizzling crackle of the lingering fires muffled the hushed sounds of our passing. An innocent pot-bellied pig lay on its side, grotesquely swollen and roasting amidst the glowing embers of what must have been its pen and straw bedding. With all its hair burned off, it was the color and texture of a football. Somehow, the hole in the back of its head where a bullet had entered was not passageway enough to release the gasses that inflated it. I watched, waiting for it to explode. It didn't so I moved on.

One of the hooches was still standing and only partially burned. Dutch pulled out that new Zippo and tried to finish the job, but the thatched roof would not take the flame. He gave up the effort when the lighter began to burn his fingers.

The bodies of an old man and two women came into view. As I drew closer, I could see the old man's wispy white beard in bold contrast to his traditional but ragged black pajamas. The Vietnamese did not appear to age until they were about fifty, when they went straight to looking ninety. He lay still, flat on his back, legs and arms splayed out slightly as if issuing a relaxed beckoning me to come even closer. He was propped up against a low embankment appropriately maintaining the dignity of his elder stature. He seemed unhurt. A serene wax figure with a zombie's thousand-yard stare. T.J. shattered my reverie when he fired his .45 into the corpse. The body shuddered a little as the bullet bored a small hole into the lower belly. A circle of lifeless blood surfaced onto his pants.

On my left, the heat waves and smoke formed a gossamer veil between the bodies of the two women and me. They had fallen close to one another near what once had been the doorway to their hooch. Although they were about twenty feet away from me, I could see that fire had burned their hair and clothes completely. Blackened skin, fissured by miniature volcanic rivers of rust-colored magma, struggled to contain the bloating gasses of decay. Each of us walked by in turn, mutely absorbing the scene. As if to ensure the full sensory impact would be welded deep into my memory, the breeze changed course again and transported to me the stench of burning hair and flesh. I don't know if it was the reeking smell or the sight of the killing that churned the bile in my stomach toward my throat.

We caught up to the Third Platoon later that afternoon in a wide field of waist-high grass. No one spoke a word into the stagnant air and debilitating heat. We knew what they had done and they knew we had seen it. Free-fire zone. These were the rules of engagement. Vulture and I chose the two locations for our gun emplacements and our squads busied themselves with the assembly and aiming of the guns. Then I found a small hollow away from the other men and drew my arms and legs tight into my body, trying to keep my emotions from spilling out.

Later, T.J. guided me over to a gathering of Charley Company grunts. They encircled two small Vietnamese men, boys really, clad only in black shorts, blindfolded, and bound at their ankles. Lengths of thin rope cinched their hands and elbows taut behind their backs.

One of the grunts offered a cursory explanation for all gathered. "Fucking VC from that ville back there. Prisoners of war."

The prisoners had no boots, no helmets, no rifles, no flak jackets, and no mortars to protect them. They were the people we were devoting our lives to killing. They had to be the enemy. They were captured in a free-fire zone.

As he sweep-kicked the legs out from under one of the prisoners, a Charley Company Marine growled, "That's for those land mines you bastards planted." Repeating his kick on the other prisoner, he barked a condemnation for the murder of his best friend. "That's for Becker, you asshole. For Becker."

The naming reverberated with both the reverence of a eulogy and the finality of a sentencing hearing. The two boys fell next to one another on their backs in the soft grass. They clamped their jaws and struggled to sit up.

A tension as tangible as static electricity before a summer thunderstorm crawled across my scalp. My knees wobbled, the muscles in my shoulders tensed, and the hair on the back of my neck bristled. All eyes bore down on the two of them. Another grunt fired a load of spit in the face of one of the prisoners. "Bastards!" he snarled. The prisoners' mouths and cheeks scrunched up like prunes.

I tried to conjure up a vision of some horrific evil so I could match my fellow Marines' wrath, so I could share their rage, their pleasurable revenge. So I could stomach what was happening. I thought of John Kitson, my friend from boot camp, a thin, scrappy New Yorker with a whiny voice but tough spirit. I pictured his face and body shredded by the Bouncing Betty land mine he triggered while walking point during his second month in Vietnam. The effort provided only a momentary distraction and failed to fuel my rage. The prisoners remained kids, scared to death, actors in the surreal stage performance playing out before me.

Revenge rose to a boil around me, swelling up like the little pig I had seen earlier in the day, ready to explode. Another Charley Company Marine came close, took a deep drag on his cigarette, and dropped to one knee to gain the right angle for pressing it into the sole of the foot of one prisoner. I think the young man smelled the effect before he felt it through the thick calluses on his bare foot. It was a slow fuse to a bomb. His explosive scream marked the moment when the burn reached nerves. A scream needs no translation. It broke the resolve of the other prisoner who probably had heard about our capabilities for cruelty. The wiry muscles in his arms and legs twitched spasmodically while his nostrils flared with rapid, shallow breaths in an attempt to control his palpable terror.

From behind me, "Hard-core. Fucking hard-core."

Then a third Marine deliberately lit up a Marlboro, knelt down on the left side of the second prisoner, and buried his cigarette into the prisoner's thigh. It was T.J. No fuse this time. The young man immediately jerked away from the searing heat, reared his head back, threw his mouth fully open and pierced the air with an animal howl. T.J. twisted to his right and threw his full body weight across the prisoner's midsection, pinning him to the ground with his greater mass. While the young man struggled, grimacing in pain, T.J. took another premeditated drag. The tip rekindled, he ground it into the prisoner's thigh at a point a little higher than the last.

A line of ants marched lock-step in the sand in front of me, responding only to the hive mentality. A giddy, out-of-body sensation freed me to float away although the interminable wails glued my boots to the soft Vietnamese soil. A bead of sweat trickled a cool line down the center of my back. My stomach grew painfully tight and my vision blurred with the turmoil of inconsistent doctrines. In an earlier life on a completely different planet, I answered at the age of thirteen what I then believed to be a divine vocation to become a Catholic priest, a saver of souls. At St. Charles Borromeo Seminary in Cleveland, I learned that Jesus taught his followers to love their enemies. Six years later, the Marines indoctrinated me to hate, to kill. The War gave me the opportunity to act out my shadow self in the name of duty and under the prophylactic excuses of "survival" and the defense, "I was merely following orders." Boot camp was supposed to inoculate me against pangs of conscience but another scream and yet another smelling salt of burning flesh made me wonder if scarring those two boys was not, in fact, what we were doing to our own souls.

I followed neither the military nor the religious doctrine. I did nothing but try to scuff a rock out of the ground with my foot. My own cowardice and fear of embarrassment paralyzed me. My instincts were those of sheep and lemmings. I chose silence as the course of least resistance and let T.J. and the other two Marines burn the boys up and down their legs and chest, a dozen places each. It took a couple of minutes. It took forever.

Lt. Smith burst into the circle of consent, his barnacled face red with rage, and with an entire lung full of breath, he fired a one-word order into each of us.

"HALT!"

That is all it took. The madness of the moment halted.

However, it was not over yet. Charley Company's Third Platoon gathered around the two prisoners for pictures. T.J. called the rest of our mortar section over too. We came together, the conquerors and the conquered. Some Marines next to me stomped the prisoners' hands and feet to the ground with their boots and others kneed them in their backs.

Standing tall directly behind the young men, I grinned for the picture. As shutters clicked, I flicked the ash of my Camel upon the black mopped head of one boy; my symbolic burning, my silent assent.

12

Internal Wars: Fire Support Base Puller; July 1969 and March 1970

From the Halls of Montezuma,
To the shores of Tripoli;
We fight our country's battles
In the air, on land, and sea;
First to fight for right and freedom
And to keep our honor clean;
We are proud to claim the title of
United States Marine.

—The Marines' Hymn (first of three verses)

Retreat! Hell, retreat's for the Army and civilians. Marines are too
damn proud to retreat."

—Senior Drill Instructor Staff sergeant Martinez in response to a
recruit's question about retreat; USMC Recruit Depot, Parris Island,
1968

Soldiers often describe war as unending boredom interspersed with moments of utter chaos. Many a soldier's relief valves are drinking and fighting. In Vietnam, booze didn't build bridges, it fueled antagonisms. There were ample clashes to choose from: Blacks versus Whites versus Hispanics, officers versus enlisted men, Southerners versus Yankees, salty Marines versus cherry Marines. For many, the break from fighting the VC was fighting each other. I had three fist fights in Vietnam: Lose, win, and draw. All were with Blacks.

Lose

I had just completed my hourly radio check from my night guard duty post high in a tower on the north end of the fire support base. The Marine on duty at the Fire Operations Center reported the time and temperature. Vietnam had cooled a full dozen degrees to a balmy eighty-five. There was a blessing from the north, a steady wind that blew the mosquitoes and biting gnats away from my face. I watched for intruders as I panned the barren landscape for movement with a Starlight night vision scope. Images of the few surviving bushes and small trees took on a ghostly green shimmer through the heavy monocle. They moved of their own accord, out of synch with my smooth sweeping action. A split second behind, they jerked to catch up. I saw the loose spiraling braids of concertina wire laced with taut strands of barbed wire stapled to posts that stood poised like Pigmy sentries. I spotted the trip flares and the Claymore mines mounted on the posts and in the sand. About fifty feet beyond lay an outer perimeter that was a duplicate in design. All seemed in order.

In line with my guard tower was a protective berm that surrounded the base. Any intruder who could possibly make it through the double rows of perimeter wire and mines would have to then survive the scramble over the berm and its exposure to a clear line of fire. Every thirty feet or so, sandbag bunkers housed Marines on guard duty with the military's most lethal weapon—the machine gun. Behind each bunker were one or two cots where off-duty guards caught a few hours of sleep before their next four-hour watch.

The defenses looked impossible to penetrate. The enemy knew otherwise. Sappers with zeal and Kamikaze courage well beyond my paltry muster had breached the barriers several times. There were blind spots between the towers and the bunkers, and beyond the range of the Starlight scopes.

Sometimes guards fall asleep. I did once. Only hours after returning to the fire support base following two weeks humping it in mountains on Operation Durham Peak, I drew guard duty. I was so pissed off and tired I just did not care what happened. In boot camp, Staff sergeant Martinez preached that sleeping on guard duty was one of the most serious crimes a soldier could commit, a capital offense. Nonetheless, people did it and nobody executed them.

I was not sleeping this night. I was fully alert to the beauty of war-torn Vietnam. Swinging the Starlight slowly through the heavens, I enjoyed the green star-tracks that arced away from my movement. I moved to the rear of the tower and scaled down the scope's power as I focused on the cold brilliance of the near-full moon. It came into view with a flare of green-gray light that filled the entire magnifying eyepiece. Although the diversion temporarily blew the night vision circuits in my viewing eye, the cosmic treat was worth it.

Silence is relative. In a noisy room full of people and ambient noise, a halt in conversation creates a palpable and uncomfortable silence. The silence of a guard tower in the middle of the night, fifty feet above the ground, one hundred feet beyond the nearest on-duty grunt, is layers deeper.

The wind brought the crackling sound of small arms fire from the tree line about two hundred yards directly north of my position. No need for the Starlight. I could see green and yellow tracer rounds arc out of the treetops in opposite directions. In an amazingly short time a gunship arrived, "Puff the Magic Dragon." Since the AC-47 was designed as a cargo plane, its large wings and lift allowed it to almost float like a chopper. Its Gatling-like 7.62 mm mini-gun, that could fire 6,000 rounds per minute, washed the trees with a red beam of destruction.

The airplane dropped illumination canisters to help its gunners distinguish friend from foe. Fortunately, I was not peering through the night vision scope when the first phosphorus torches flared with two hundred thousand candle-power of blinding light. As the flares slowly drifted down on their big parachutes during the three-minute burn time, they made the forms below dance in an other-worldly, blue-gray glow. Even at a distance, I heard the faint high-pitched whistle made by the fast-escaping gases.

The smell of thermite, gunpowder, and still-burning phosphorus mixed with the ripe, dank smells of the jungle. The war was a beautiful thing when I was not participating. I enjoyed the dazzling grandeur of the most technologically advanced super-power in history trying to blow away a little Third World nation.

The gunship pilot must have miscalculated the strength of the wind because one of the illumination rounds wafted directly toward my guard tower. The intense blue-white flare quieted to a glowing red ember atop the three-foot high silvery canister. Its acrid smoke engulfed my perch as the huge parachute loomed ever larger. The chute reflected its own pale blue-gray glow as it encompassed the full spectrum of my peripheral vision. Incredibly, it blanketed the entire top of the tower and formed a silk cocoon for me.

As I thought of how wonderful the parachute would be to send home, I heard a gruff command from below, "It's mine!"

I walked curiously to the left of the tower and peered down. A dark hulk gathered the lines near where the canister had landed. "The hell it is!" I retorted with bold abandon into the darkness. As he pulled on the nylon lines from below, I gathered silk from above. "Drop it, asshole," I shouted. The tug-of-war abruptly stopped and I hurriedly pulled the rest of the silk into the tower. Then my nest began to shake as I felt him coming up the ladder.

Maybe it was the violent shake of the tower. Maybe it was this looming view as he topped the ladder and strode toward me. He was

easily six inches taller than me and had the tumescent chest of a
weight lifter. Maybe it was his sergeant stripes. Maybe it was his race.
Whatever. Fear paralyzed me. The big man stepped right up into my
face and spoke four words through clenched teeth that gleamed in the
moonlight.

"Mine, you honky bastard!"

He grabbed the chute with his left hand and yanked it and me
toward him. His right fist slammed square into the bridge of my nose
with crushing force. There was a moment of time I do not remember
while I careened eight feet back to the side wall of the tower. One
instant I was facing this man-mountain, the next I was crumpled on
my side with a profusely bleeding nose and lip. I sensed no pain but
stayed there, flash frozen into a posture of utter defeat. My courage
was stillborn, DOA.

"Move, and I will gouge your eyes out and skull-fuck you, asshole."

He delivered the threat with clipped words and a sneer of derision
on his face. With a quick slice of the nylon lines with his K-Bar, he
gathered the silken prize and completed his mission. He left, shaking
the ladder and tower as defiantly on his descent as on his ascent.

I recalled Staff sergeant Martinez delivering that same threat to a
demoralized recruit in boot camp. It was funny then. Lying cowed on
the floor of that tower, I was glad my drill instructor was not there to
watch me retreat from the intruder.

Win

When I had only four weeks remaining in my tour of duty, T.J.
cracked. A simple bureaucratic error on the rotation lists was the final
straw. Each day, Headquarters staff posted a list of Marines whose
tours of duty would be up in the next week. Those to rotate home that
day headed the list. Short-timers made a daily ritual of checking the
list and watching their names climb toward the top. T.J. was ready to

leave. He was over-ripe. The day he was to rotate home his name magically disappeared from the top of the list. I was with him when he stormed into the Headquarters bunker and raged at the first clerk he found. Wisely, the clerk told him that it was just an unfortunate mistake and that they would correct it the next day. "You will be on the Freedom Bird tomorrow, Corporal. In the meantime, go get drunk." T.J. spent the rest of the day in the Enlisted Men's (EM) Club following the clerk's suggestion.

I heard the rest of the story from Scrounger. When T.J.'s name was still missing from the list the next day he marched slowly into the Headquarters bunker, drew his .45, and chambered a round with a smooth, well-practiced sweep of his left hand. The solid metallic double-click sound of the pistol grabbed everyone's attention. When he found the clerk who had put him off the day before, he carefully aimed the pistol at the clerk's head and fired this conclusion at him: "I am going home today. Try telling me I'm not, Private."

"Yes you are, Corporal." What else could he say?

T.J. did leave that day and with no other consequences for his threat. I got his job as Section Leader of the Second Section. My primary responsibility was mortar training for the cherry Marines, fresh in country. My Commanding Officer also told me to revamp the guard duty roster for the entire mortar platoon. People had been complaining of the inequities in the old schedule so I jumped at the opportunity and designed a logical program that was equitable for all...well, almost everyone. I happened to have scheduled Pvt. Washington to serve two nights with only one day off between. He was the last to serve on the old roster and one of the first to serve on mine. It just worked out that way.

The night I posted the guard roster for the next two weeks, Washington had been drinking at the EM Club. Later, he came looking for me with a few of his friends. He found Long John and me outside our hooch and began to complain in a loud voice slurred by alcohol. As I calmly explained the logic of my duty roster and its long-term fairness, a small crowd gathered around us, including some of my trainees. I smelled Washington's hot, alcohol-scented breath as his much taller form drew closer. His eyes scowled with anger. We all sought revenge against an invisible enemy that constantly threatened with hidden mines and snipers, sporadic rockets, and untrustworthy civilians; against a war that corroded our spirits; against superiors who made dubious decisions that risked our lives. Washington's rage had the additional fuel of suspected racism.

"You honky, white mothers always got it in for us brothers, don't you! Keep the nigger behind the trigger, right?"

My senses, fueled by adrenaline, went on full alert, the classic fight-or-flight response. "Keep your shit together, Washington." I took a small step forward with my left foot to balance my weight on the balls of my feet. "Don't be making no big mistake here now."

His drunkeness slowed his moves and telegraphed his intentions. There was very little light so I sensed his fist heading for my face before I saw it clearly. I ducked to my left and Washington's unimpeded thrust carried him one step closer to me with his right arm fully extended over my right shoulder.

My body took over instinctively and initiated hand-to-hand combat moves well practiced from boot camp but intended for the enemy. I shot my right knee up and into Washington's now-exposed groin. He belched eighty-proof air along with a deep groan. As he began to double over, my right arm whipped across so that my bony elbow drove right into Washington's face. His head jerked back from the blow and his entire body crumpled as he dropped, slightly spinning, toward the ground. He landed askew and rolled uncontrollably onto his back and up against my left foot. I was on automatic pilot. Disconnected from my body, my legs collapsed on their own and my right knee brought most of my 120 pounds square into his stomach. His face involuntarily jerked up toward me and wheezed all reserve air. With a blind passion I did not know was in me, my left fist hammered his face savagely back into the sand. My upper body followed through to the right and then uncoiled in an even more forceful right cross to his face. My body found a rhythm as I drummed Washington with both fists. He offered no resistance. After four or five staccato punches, Long John dragged me off before my fury was spent. Washington's friends helped him back to consciousness and dragged him away into the night. "I will Article-15 your ass!" I shouted triumphantly after him.

Since I was a corporal, a non-commissioned officer, Washington's attack was an offense that warranted a court-marshal. I could have written him up for it, and he could have served time or, more likely, received a mark on his service record. I saw no use in that. Instead, I approached him the next day to try to explain how my roster was based on logic, not racism, and that my intentions were unbiased. He would hear nothing of it. His face was severely swollen, left eye was closed shut, and lip was split. He turned and stomped away from me so I abandoned the idea of convincing him.

Draw

The issue of the guard duty roster was not over yet. It fomented more racial strife. The third round of my service fights occurred a short time later, on a late morning just as the sun was firing up for another blistering day. I had finished a training session with the cherry Marines and had stripped down to a pair of jungle shorts and my boonie hat to rest with some tunes in the shade. Pvt. Ames approached me. He had just come off guard duty and said that my new system was unfair to him, too. He was a handsome man and still dressed in full utilities, helmet, boots, flak jacket, and his .45 Cal. pistol. I told him I did my best to make it fair to everyone and that I singled no one out for extra duty.

I stood up, faced his over six-foot frame, and asked what his specific complaint was. His sculptured face radiated fury at that moment, probably due to having spent the last hours of his watch blaming me for the systemic racism all around him. This time when that right jab came, it was not slowed by alcohol. Like the first fight I had in the guard tower, I regained self-awareness some six feet distant. This time, however, I did not cower. I leapt to my feet and crazily jumped at his shoulders shoving both of us back against the sand-bagged wall of the Fire Operations Center. Before I could do anything effective, he pealed me off him with a powerful shove and threw me five feet back into the sand. Enraged, I flew at him a second time. He bent over to absorb my attack and grabbed my right arm. In one fluid motion, he flipped me over his back and onto the sand again. Before I could launch a third totally ineffective attack, people dragged me away. Others pushed him out of the area as well and the incident was over.

Here I was, trained by the Marines in hand-to-hand combat, proud of knowing several ways to maim and kill with my bare hands. Instead of engaging this knowledge, I created a new fighting style that could best be labeled as "leaping for self-injury." Cowardice was unacceptable. You had to fight, especially when there was no chance of winning, even if you risked making a fool of yourself.

13

Paranoia Strikes Deep: Fire Support Base Puller; March 1970

And we cannot help but come away with an image of war as one of the most horrifying and traumatic events a human being can participate in. War is an environment that will psychologically debilitate ninety-eight percent of all who participate in it for any length of time. And the two percent who are not driven insane by war appear to have already been insane—aggressive psychopaths—before coming to the battlefield.

—Lt. Col. Dave Grossman, *On Killing: The Psychological Cost of Learning to Kill in War and Society*

You're so short, you had better wear a raincoat in case the ants piss on you.

—Long John

Killer Competition

When I was a short-timer, I mean *really short*, as in less than three weeks remaining in my tour of duty, the ever-present, background anxiety began to grow in me like a tumor. The shorter my time remaining, the more paranoid I became. I was convinced my number had to come up. I figured my life was a loan that was funded by the death and destruction all around me. The term on the loan was running out. I had to pay up. A USO show helped tip me over the edge.

I saw USO shows five or six times on our base when I was not in the bush. They featured Asian entertainers, mostly Vietnamese and occasionally Filipinos, doing ersatz rock and roll with thick accents that made the lyrics even less intelligible than the groups that originally performed the music. We mocked their attempts at our language and music—until the dancers came out. Then we fell instantly in love, or at least in lust. We were a tinder-dry forest that had not seen a raindrop for many, many months and they were a careless match. Whenever the showgirls revealed a little thigh or cleavage, we would go wild, hooting, whistling, jumping up and down in the dust cloud, and dancing in place to match the gyrations of the temptresses. Our solicitations were in the same tongue as our body language, with little interest in formalities and introductions. Every performance escalated to the climactic point when the girls slowly stripped down to bikini underwear during a slinky exotic dance. Inevitably, a few Marines would leap on stage to press some flesh and dance with the girls until the Military Police (MP) regained control and closed down the show. It happened that way every time, every time but once.

Word went out that a special troupe would soon visit. They would have Australian entertainers to boost the moral of their country's troops. Finally, "round-eyed" dancers. It was the monsoon season. With half of the base under water, the base engineers set up a temporary stage on the edge of the LZ the day before the big show. Long

John and I decided to get up early for the morning performance and claim good spots. I awoke first and hurriedly dressed in the damp air. I shivered in the pre-dawn light on my way to Long John's hooch. The wet ground crunched beneath my boots. Not yet awake, I was convinced that the temperature had dropped so much that the ground was beginning to freeze. I slapped the bottoms of Long John's feet to wake him and used his radio to check on the temperature. It was 65 degrees. I did the math. It was 45 degrees colder than the previous midday, the same temperature differential as between a comfortable 75 degrees and the freezing point of water. We needed something to warm our tired bones.

During the long wait for the start of the show, Long John and I fanned each other's longing to view our first Caucasian women since arriving in country. By the time nearly the entire base had crammed on to the LZ, the anticipation was at a fever pitch. Then the Australian band burst on-stage to crank out the rock and roll with a nuclear energy. Soon they had us all pumped up and dancing together to a hard driving rendition of Steppenwolf's "Born to be Wild:" "Get your motor running. Head out on the highway looking for adventure in whatever comes our way. Yeah, darling gonna make it happen, take the world in a love embrace. Fire all your guns at once and explode into space. Like a true nature child we were born—born to be wild. We have climbed so high, never want to die. Born to be wild."

Midway through the first verse, two statuesque blondes strutted onto the stage to take over the background singing. Dancing to the beat, they wore matching white go-go boots, micro-miniskirts, and tank tops that looked two sizes too small for their envious jobs. We screamed our war whoops in an orgasmic welcome.

After fanning our frenzy further with the Troggs' "Wild Thing," they settled us down with a sentimental take on the Beatles' "Hey Jude," singing it with the patriotic fervor of a national anthem. The girls' golden hair reminded me of my Bridget back home, but given the intensity of the moment, I was one of hundreds who would have married either of the singers on the spot. To my delight, they closed the show with the song that I used as a mantra to get through boot camp, "Sunshine of Your Love" by Cream. They ran off the stage and did not respond to our incessant screams for an encore. They had another gig at the next Marine base on Hill 55.

With the music still sparking through my nervous system, I walked with several others to the backstage area hoping to exchange addresses with the women that would sing to me in my dreams. I thought I had found the perfect pen pals, but the MPs ordered us away.

After our show, they never had the chance to write to me or anyone else. The VC ambushed their convoy on the road to Hill 55. Both women died.

Short Enough to Go in a Hole Without Even Ducking

Somehow, those deaths hit me harder than the deaths of the men in my unit. We were soldiers. Death was part of the bargain. The myopic formula in my mind was that the men go off to war to protect their women from the enemy. It did not seem fair. I went into a deep slump for days after the news. I thought of writing Bridget but did not want to burden her with my foul mood. I sent off a short letter to Cynthia, my Empire State Building confidant, and told her how the death of people who were not supposed to die added to my paranoia that my number had to be up soon. I had dodged my last bullet. Writing helped but I still could not shake the feeling. That's when Long John came to the rescue with a clear plan of action.

"You zonked out, man? OK, J.M., we'll go underground. If the slopes can survive underground, so can we."

Without hesitation, we set to work, first doing a low crawl through the thirty-inch space between the ground and the center of the wooden platform of our hooch. Instead of our rifles, we cradled entrenching tools and armfuls of empty plastic sandbags. The floor joists harbored all kinds of many-legged creatures.

"Watch for the widows, man," Long John warned.

"Shit! I should have warn a cover," I said while brushing the dusty cobwebs and desiccated globs of web-encased prey from my hair. We swept an area of flooring clear of crawlies and set to the task of filling sandbags from the prone position. Long John kept banging his lanky arms against the floor joists.

"J.M., did I ever tell you what we did to the CO when he was cherry?"

"Something just crawled over your leg, Long John. No. Tell me."

"Well, you see, he started this routine of snap inspections at oh-six-hundred. This dude had our asses up in the early a.m.—guard duty or no—for some lifer drill. And he'd latrine-duty any poor sucker who failed. Dig this, we had to shine our boots."

"No shit! How can you tell how salty a man is with shined boots?"

"Fuckin' A. My point exactly. Something had to be done."

"Whaddya do, frag him?"

"Well, Vulture came up with this plan. The first night we snagged this black widow—a big mother—put it in a baggie…"

"Where'd you find her?"

"On the trap door to the shitters. Anyway, we put her in an empty can of beans-and-mother-fuckers and taped the baggie over the mouth. Vulture rolled it under the side flaps of the CO's hooch. You could hear it bang against the leg of the cot so I'm sure it woke him up."

"So you expected a hard-ass Marine officer to change his mind 'cause you interrupted his wet dream with a spider?"

"That was Day One, my man. Day One. Now, Day Two we rolled another can under his cot, but this one had three of these black beauties and the baggie had little rips in it."

"I get it, not big enough for the creepies to get out but big enough to make the poor bastard **think** some may have gotten out." Long John held the sand bag open as I shoveled a three-pound load of Vietnam into it.

"Right on, right on, college boy. But it still didn't work. So, we commenced Day Three. Vulture and I sneaked up to the tent, this is twenty-hundred hours or so, and Vulture does his routine. Only this time the C-rat can's got no baggie at all. We roll it as usual under his cot, make a noise and didi-mau our asses outta' there."

"OK, radio man, were your eight-legged friends scarier by their presence or their absence?" We were running out of space to store the full sand bags. A wall grew up faster than the hole grew down, cutting off the flow of cool air. It did not matter. Long John's story provided the cool breeze that drove the doldrums from my spirits.

"Don't know," he admitted. "My section got tagged for another op. Another two-week search-and-destroy mission. Hey, at least there were no inspections in the bush."

"Roger that one. I've actually volunteered my Second Section for operations and bush time to avoid the piddly-ass, bullshit in the rear."

"J.M.! Watch out for that centipede by your left arm!"

A quick flick of the E-tool and I cut the three-inch insect into two squirming half-lives of confusion. "Hell, that was just the baby. I'll tell you about the papa-san centipede, Long John. The King Kong of centipedes." We needed our stories to connect us—to prop up our humanity. It takes two to tell a story. "Once upon a time when I was rebuilding the old gun pit at the Han Song bridge position…"

"This better be a true story, J.M. I don't want you to waste your bullshit on a bug story."

"The truth. I swear it over Chesty Puller's grave," I said. "Besides, you'll know when I lie. My face will go as red as a baboon's butt."

The sweat from every pore mixed with Vietnam's fine dirt to make us into mud-encased moles. We melded with the dirt to beat the odds of the "dust-to-dust" prediction.

"So I was ripping open the old rotten sandbags when this centipede crawled out just a few inches from my hand. I do my jump-back-Jack when I see this monster's more than a foot long."

"Don't you shit me now, J.M. They taught you not to lie to your radioman in the seminary, didn't they?"

"I would re-up for another tour with my beloved Corps before I'd lie to you, Sparks. This slithering bastard was slow. Moved just like a snake but with a bazillion jet-black legs. Each one was an inch long and moved in a wave like the Rockettes. Now you know how some animals use camouflage to avoid predators."

"Yeah, like the VC avoid us."

"Exactly. Well, this bad mother has an inch-wide body that's bright orange and red, and a huge black head with a pair of pincers the size of hawk's claw. He's screaming 'Try takin' me on.' He probably tastes as bad as you smell."

"So being the bad-ass Marine you are, I suppose you engaged him in hand-to-hand, and then slapped the naked-death-strangle-hold on him until he promised to whistle the Marine Corps Hymn while saluting the flag with fifty right feet." As Long John delivered his harangue, he began dragging the thirty-pound sandbags along the twenty-foot pathway we had cleared of webs to the edge of the hooch. We would need them later to fill in the space between the roof of the bunker and the floor of the hooch.

"I wish. No, he got away before I could grab my E-tool and I didn't want to go looking for him. I'm sure his cousins live around here." I could not stop my incessant chatter. Anything to avoid thinking about the war. In spite of my growing tiredness from hard work in cramped quarters, I felt an urgency to get the bunker completed.

"You never met Schlotter," I continued. "Cool dude from Philadelphia. Pretty good on the guitar and one hell of a fast gunner. He was a squad leader for the First Section. Well, a centipede bit him on the upper lip one night. He woke up screaming so loud half the base went on alert."

"Far out, man. What happened to him?"

"They medevaced him to the hospital in Da Nang. We heard he almost died."

"Might have been worth it if he didn't have to come back here."

"Oh, they sent him back but the swelling and blue color never left his face. He lost his edge so they reassigned him to stay 'in the rear with the gear.' Vulture got his job."

"Hell of a way to get promoted, J.M. I wonder if that's how Vulture came up with his spider-in-a-can idea."

We dug the pit six feet down. The digging got easier when we could kneel and then stand up, but the drain of having to drag the hundreds of bags away made me appreciate the life of the Vietnamese tunnelers. We quit when the hole was eight by six feet in size. For the roof, Scrounger scavenged a couple of the perforated steel plates designed for LZs. It was strong enough to support the two feet of sandbags that we piled on top. We accessed the bunker down a narrow side ramp that was hidden from view and protected by grenade pits. We added an emergency trap-door exit out the other end. Our air vents were impossible to spot. After piling excess dirt around the sandbags on the roof and ramped entrance, the bunker was completely hidden. To a person curious enough to look under the hooch, it looked as if the hooch sat atop a simple mound of dirt.

Long John decided it was time for a break from the digging and he had another plan. "I noticed you got another one of those packages from the states yesterday. Full of pogey bait isn't it? Cough some up, Jack, for your radioman."

"My dear sweet mother volunteered her precious time so that I would have a little comfort in this hell-hole. She don't give a rat's ass about you, so I don't see why I should give you jack-shit, Jack."

"Well, do I really need to remind you how many times I saved your ass in the bush by calling in back-up artillery? Or the time I snuck in a whore for the entire platoon? How 'bout when I…"

"Ok, Ok. I'll get the package." I didn't tell him I had nothing to do with the prostitute. Mom's group, called We Do Care, sent monthly packages to local service personnel. These "CARE" packages brimmed with treats; supplies we couldn't always get like toothpaste, socks and underwear; and newspaper articles about local happenings. The centerpiece of that month's treat was a dozen oatmeal raisin cookies, triple-wrapped in aluminum foil. We ate every one of them and washed them down with a couple of warm beers that Long John had stashed away.

Even before we completed our sanctuary, we decided to seek a night's refuge in it. In the middle of the night, the sound of somebody screaming put me on full alert. I awoke, bathed in a cold sweat and a feeling of doom, sweeping the dark space with the loaded .45 Cal. pistol that was my constant companion. Long John was having one of his nightmares. I found the souls of his boots and kicked them to bring him back from the dream war to the real one. "J.M., I was dead and buried and had a bad fever on top of it." People often get premonitions when they have to do jobs that can get them killed.

"Do you believe in God, J.M.?" There was plenty of time there to think about life's big issues.

"You know what they say, Long John. There are no atheists in a fox hole."

"Fine, but what does that mean to you?"

I told him that it was the logical outcome of a religion based on fear of punishment and hope for afterlife rewards. War was supposed to be the ultimate test of belief. The fires of war would burn away the trivial and expose the soul.

"Fine, but do you pray, J.M.?"

I leveled with him. I said that I had survived the fiery test, burrowed into the ground in terror, quaked at the sight of bodies blown apart by my own mortar rounds. Yet, I never once felt driven to my knees to plead with the God of my youth for deliverance from the evil I witnessed and took part in.

"I was raised Southern Baptist, J.M., but I tired of religious bullies and eventually outgrew it." He lit up a Lucky. "I still believe in God though." By this time I was wide awake and ready to pass the time with a little philosophy. Long John continued, "Ever hear about the theory where if you've got two or more explanations for something, the shortest one is the best?"

I thought about it, and dredged up the answer from my high school physics class. I told him the theory he was referring to is called Ockham's Razor. Ockham said that in the case where multiple theories explain a phenomenon equally well, the simplest is probably correct.

"OK, J.M., on the one hand you got a God that created the universe and takes an active role in keeping it all in good working order. This is the same God that I can pray to and maybe, if I pray real hard and believe in him deep down, he'll spare me for another day here. In fact if I pray harder than you, the next incoming round will smoke your ass instead of mine."

"Not if I believe harder and hit the dirt faster, Long John."

"Well," he continued, "we'll call that Case A: There is a God."

"And he's a busy one," I quipped in.

"Now Case B will be no God at all. Here we got the whole universe popping out of nowhere."

"Evolving," I corrected him.

"I got a problem…"

"It's OK, you can get shots from the medic."

"Listen up, smart ass," Long John said taking back the conversation with his raspy voice. "Where-it's-at is all this creation and no creator. It's just too unbelievable. It's too unfucking believably complex to imagine the entire universe coming into being on its own. Creation creating itself. So Ockham's Razor would favor the existence of God."

I argued the opposite case: "Both Case A and Case B rely on the idea of a creation without a creator. Ockham's theory would favor the simpler of the two. So, which is simpler, a universe that can create itself, your Case B, or an entity that can create the creator of the universe, your Case A? Ockham's Razor cuts the balls off your argument, Long John."

We had plenty of time to debate the matter and ended up agreeing on only one thing that Long John articulated well. "God doesn't give a shit about us. I believe he started things in the beginning but he sure as hell isn't here now in any real way. If you want to pick the simplest explanation for the evil out there, you don't need to believe in an outside force.

You know the excuse, 'the Devil made me do it.' There's more than enough badness in human nature to explain the evil in the world."

I ventured the final word: "So I guess Ockham's Razor lets God off the hook and keeps us hanging on it." Long John agreed. Although my dog-tags have the word "Catholic" stamped permanently into them, I had stopped thinking of myself as a Christian long before that night deep in my bunker fortress.

Then my friend bumped the conversation in a little different direction. "If you studied for four years to become a priest, how is it you've come to be an Atheist?"

"Whoa. Don't take my love of debate too far," I countered. "I'm not convinced either way. I don't think we're capable of knowing."

"Agnostic, then."

"Probably."

"I'll say again, J.M., what pushed you from being a Catholic and a seminarian to an Agnostic?"

"Oh, that's easy. Sex."

"You better tell me this story."

"Well, if you want to know how I got from there to here, it was like dominoes tipping over in a curving line. My parents were the first dominoes. They raised me with a lot of love and clear direction to be a good Catholic. That steered me to the seminary high school, the second domino. After four terrific years there…"

"What about the 'sex' part?"

"I'm coming to that. I was seventeen and near the end of my senior year before I fully realized I couldn't hack a life of celibacy. I knew I wanted a normal life with a family so I dropped out of the seminary after graduation, went to Kent State University and started dating in college. That's when I met Bridget. She's the next domino that fell."

Secure in our bunker, I felt it was safe to ignore Wild Bill's sage advice against fantasizing. I remembered how, with the sanctions of our burgeoning "free-love" subculture, we launched our own personal sexual revolution. Bridget served as the copilot of my rebellion. I told Long John how Bridget and I, both Catholics and virgins when we met, started down the path of sex, taking small steps at first. Attraction developed into friendship, friendship to my first intimate touches. Petting led to passion and from there to an infatuation that burned with an intensity only inexperienced lovers can generate. Fortunately, the nuns and priests had so much difficulty talking about sex, they skipped over the wide range of sexual possibilities and focused only on the dirtiest of deeds, the neutron bomb of mortal sins that would blast you straight to Dante's lowest level of Hell: Sexual intercourse. This moral Maginot Line reserved a lot of other territory for exploration at the manageable price of venial sins and a temporary sentence in the afterlife fires of Purgatory. Our souls dangled by the thinnest of threads to the belief systems of our birth legacy.

My virginity was settling in hard on me. After four months of incrimentalism, the sole remaining step seemed small and natural. What seemed unnatural was having to perform the Orwellean trick of doublethink and accept both the Church's notion that the same God that would create us in his image and make us capable of a love so enrapturing would also condemn us to Hell. I told Long John about the episode that ended up charting whole chapters of my life.

The seminal event took place nine months before I went into the service. It was during the Christmas holidays in 1968 after Bridget and I spent our first three months together at Kent State University. We cooked up a plan to spend our first night together at my trailer. Bridget told her parents she would be staying with me for three days at my parents' home, and I told my parents I would be staying the first night with Bridget and her family, and then we would both come there for the next two days. Everything went according to plan, at first. We had a rapturous night of lovemaking. We were oblivious to the snow that blanketed Northeast Ohio. A thrown pillow muffled the clock's morning alarm. The simple courtesy of a phone call within the next hour to tell my parents that we would be a little late would have set matters on a different course, but I wasn't concerned with phone courtesy. We set out for Cleveland with a late start and a driving speed slowed to a crawl by the near blizzard conditions.

Worried about our late arrival, my mother called Bridget's parents to find out when we had left there. When we finally walked through the door, my mother's only words were "We want to talk to you both." I whispered to Bridget that they must know and that there was no sense lying.

What followed was two days of interrogation that we named "The Inquisition." First my father grilled us on the details of our actions and preached of our malefic intent.

"Do you realize how much you have hurt your mother and me? We didn't raise you to lie and sneak around us. Is that what they taught you in the seminary, to fornicate?"

I had learned as a small boy that most of my father's questions were rhetorical and were best met with stoical silence.

"We are ashamed of you. You've insulted us and made liars of us because we told Bridget's parents that no son of ours would ever do such a despicable thing. What kind of example are you setting for your younger brothers and sister?"

Somehow, Bridget held her tongue. When Dad launched on a direct attack on Bridget as the modern Whore of Babylon, I leapt to her defense. In a valiant act of adolescent chivalry, I shouldered all the blame for our actions. It was futile.

We took a brief break and Bridget escaped to the bathroom and then retreated to the guest bedroom and refused to come out until we left the next afternoon for her home. Mom spelled Dad to deliver a short but painful sermon on sin and shame to me alone. Before she finished, Father Schmidt joined the two of us. He was an aging Catholic priest who was a long-time friend of the family and was staying at the house over the holiday. He took advantage of a pause in Mom's diatribe to play the good cop role.

"Michael, this is a very serious matter. Perhaps this is a good time for me to hear your confession. Then we can begin to move forward again, fresh. What do you say to that, son?" Father Schmidt was like an unofficial member of the family. In fact, since I left home at the age of thirteen to live at the seminary, my parents probably saw more of him than me. "We're dealing with a mortal sin here, you know, Michael." He turned to my mother and added, "Let me have a moment with the boy, if you will." Presuming agreement, he concluded, "Thank you. We shouldn't be long." As Mom left he reached into the pocket of his black coat and produced a purple confessional stole that he draped around his neck. Body armor for the sins of others.

I cleared my throat with an easy admission to the more common sin of lying about our whereabouts. It bought time as I gathered my wits to deal with the mortal sin of fornication. "We love one another. Is this love a mortal sin?" I asked, mimicking my father's rhetorical style. Before the old priest could answer with a quote from the Baltimore Catechism, I advanced my case another step. "Was our first touch, or first hug a sin? How about our first kiss? Everything progressed like that from the love that we share. How do you draw a line where love ends and sin begins, Father? Where do you draw the line where venial sin ends and mortal sin begins?" I had argued many a fine theological point in the seminary with priests, but never on matters of sex and never with my faith in the balance.

Father Schmidt's demeanor changed from that of a confident patri-arch to one with a tinge of perturbation. I was not dissuaded. "To sin," I continued, the steam rising in my argument, "one has to know the commission is sinful. But it didn't feel sinful. It felt honest. It felt inno-cent; like a gift to each other. My conscience is clear. I don't have another sin to confess."

"Michael!" He interrupted my rapture with a voice stripped of its former soothing quality and stood up tall and erect to deliver his retort. He lacked only a pulpit. "You were raised Catholic by your par-ents. Good Catholics. You had the extra advantage of an excellent Catholic education. Now you expect me to believe you don't know when you've sinned? You had four years in the seminary studying to become a Catholic priest. How dare you argue that **you** have the right and authority to determine whether your fornication is a sin or not."

He didn't buy my existential sleight-of-hand. I couldn't help but picture him in the role of Dostoyevsky's "Grand Inquisitor" as he went on to defend the Church's moral imperative to fetter free will with divine mysteries and infinite rewards and punishments. "Without confession, you risk burning for all eternity in Hell. Ask God's forgiveness and heaven is your eternal reward. I'll be here when you are ready to confess your sin."

The punishment did not fit the crime. I could no longer swallow that theological candy.

He left with these last words and died two years later. I knew he cared for me and was just doing his job but I never had the chance as an adult to repair our relationship outside of the influence of the times.

Then my father returned refreshed and relentless. The overall effect was a coordinated frontal attack aimed at deprogramming us from the clutches of a cult, the diabolical anarchy of the '60s. They had the advantage, the high ground, because my parents and my church had trained me exquisitely in the fine art of obedience.

The next afternoon, Bridget's parents gave us a similar but much briefer lecture. I returned home for the rest of the three-week break to a wall of parental silence broken only by occasional refresher comments and scowls. Playing the role of the compliant and dutiful son one last time, I was silent through it all.

The incident played out in a thousand variations in a million homes around the world. Loving parents with heartfelt concern for sons and daughters tried every means at their disposal to keep the chaos of the times at bay. The more Mom and Dad tried to protect me from what they saw as the sinful decadence of the sex-drugs-and-rock-and-roll '60s, the more I craved the forbidden fruit. At the start of The Inquisition, Bridget and I were young adults enraptured in the hot but normally short-lived flame of infatuated first love. Two days later, we emerged as two people welded together by shared adversity and a common enemy on a mission to free ourselves from the oppression we perceived as endemic to our parents' generation. For the next four years, Bridget and I used The Inquisition to blame those who would keep us apart for all that we saw as wrong in the world. The convenience of an obvious enemy hid the need to examine the enemy within our relationship.

"So that's how it happened, Long John. Six months later I was still pissed at my dad so I gave him the finger by enlisting in the Marines. I figured I'd teach him a lesson if I went and got myself killed in Vietnam. Whaddya' think, Long John?…Long John?" A steady rhythm of deep breathing was the only other sound in our black cave. It wasn't the first or the last time my long ruminations put someone to sleep.

The next day, we ran power in for lights and the tape deck and a huge stereo system Long John purchased while on R & R in Bangkok. We smoked up that incredible Nam weed and cranked his stereo to the limits. Procol Harem sang to us. Janis poured her heart out for us. "Freedom's just another word for nothin' left to lose." Blood, Sweat & Tears taught us philosophy. "What goes up, must come down, spinning wheel spinning 'round. Talkin' 'bout your troubles, it's a cryin' sin, ride a painted pony, let the spinning wheel spin."

Before the service, Long John had his own radio program, "The Long John Show," for a station in his home town of Memphis. He carried his nickname to Vietnam. "I'm down, Long John. Entertain me," I'd tell him, and he would.

"Aye, me hearties," he would start in a delightful imitation of Disney's Long John Silver brogue. "Let me spin ye a yarn 'bout Mister Victor Charley and his rag-tag band o' cut-throats.…"

And this is how it went for three weeks in our bunker, me blathering away on anything that came to mind, and Long John with his monologues that wove in the folly of the War with his old radio routines. I spent all my free time in that bunker during my last three weeks in country. Together, we resisted the pull of darkness. Together, we kept the paranoia at bay.

14

Cleansing Down to the Soul: Da Nang Airport and Okinawa; March 1970

One year after flying into the Air Force base near Da Nang, I returned to that base for my flight home. A supply clerk asked respectfully for my gear. With slow deliberateness, I placed my M16 on the counter. It was as clean as the clerk's freshly scrubbed baby face. As he took down its serial number, I wondered whom it would next protect. Maybe the next Marine grunt would get the confirmed kill with it that I hadn't. He accepted my helmet, four M16 magazines, canteen, and flak jacket, and tossed the rotting jacket onto a dusty heap in the corner of the room. Finally, I stripped off my utility belt that carried my .45 Cal. pistol, holster, two ammunition clips, and my K-Bar knife. I slipped off the knife and laid the pistol on the counter. Anxiety washed over me. I recalled the fear of the unknown that haunted me during the original trip on March 17, 1969 from this base to Fire Support Base Puller and compared it to the fear of what I was so certain would happen. I could not shake the gut feeling that disaster would strike me before I could plant my feet on U.S. soil. My sense of being defenseless, exposed, and naked spoiled my appreciation of the plush new surroundings on the base: the air conditioned buildings with real beds, hot showers, flush toilets; and well-cooked food in a mess hall with chairs. I slept fitfully throughout my first unarmed night in Vietnam, awakening often in search of my missing .45 and the masculine creak of its leather holster.

The next day I boarded a commercial jet, the long-awaited "Freedom Bird," and took a seat by the window for a last look on my world before I departed for my next life. On the seat next to me was a day-old paper from the States with a banner headline emblazoned across the top declaring: "Apollo 13: Moonwalk Planned." I was too astonished to read the article just then. Ever since I was a kid, I followed the NASA adventure with great interest, right up to watching the early Apollo launches just before I went into the service.

When a flight attendant approached, I caught her attention and exclaimed, "Can you believe this!" pointing to the headline. "We're finally going to put a man on the moon and I didn't know anything about it."

Even then, I knew a lot of my success at surviving a tour in Vietnam was due to my skill at keeping focused on survival only. The stewardess did not seem to appreciate the significance of my discovery. Instead, she found my comment humorous. This was to be the **third** moon walk, she explained. The first moon walk, the one that people now remember with as much clarity as JFK's assassination, had occurred eight months earlier on July 20, 1969—while I was on a search-and-destroy mission as a part of Operation Durham Peak.

The next leg of my journey home was to Okinawa for a three-day layover. No one told me why. The very first thing I did after getting squared away in my temporary barrack was to visit the base library. I was on a new mission to get clean, really clean. It was not that we couldn't shower in Vietnam. During the summer of 1969, the artillery company rigged a makeshift shower on the firebase. I reveled in that shower, my first since arriving, and scrubbed hard to scrape the filth of war from my pores. But by the time I walked back to my hooch wrapped in a towel, I was again coated in sweat and fine yellow dust.

Worse yet, my cleanliness must have been a beacon for the mosquitoes and biting flies. I learned that a layer of grime was better protection than the mosquito repellent available and I returned to the former practice of occasional splash baths using my helmet as a basin. As a compromise, I focused on keeping just one part of me clean, my teeth. I kept a toothbrush encased in a little plastic bag in my tunic so I could give the pearlies a wash several times a day.

The dirt and grime of Vietnam had penetrated deep into me and I wanted it out. Before I left, Vulture mentioned how India's yogis used salt water cleansing techniques for the total body and I wanted desperately to learn how to do them. The base librarian on Okinawa steered me to just the right book, complete with pictures and short enough for me to scan in its entirety in one sitting. Thereafter, I began a regular practice of mixing salt and warm water to the approximate concentration of sea water and snorting it up and then out of my nose. The book's author used the example of human tears and blood having the same salinity as sea water as an illustration of the inter-linking of all of creation.

The next afternoon, I was killing time in the barrack with two other Marines when I heard someone say, "J.M.! How the hell are you?" I first noticed the small gold crosses in his shirt lapels. It was Capt. Philip Hanson. As we gingerly shook hands, I noticed how he had changed in appearance since he served as the chaplain for Fire Support Base Puller in Vietnam. The mid-day light streaming in through the Quonset hut windows gleamed off the shiny, tanned skin of his high, wide forehead. I didn't remember him being so bald. His entreating smile and inviting gaze reminded me of the authentic sincerity he extended to me whenever I had seen him in country. As I introduced him to my new friends, I noticed how he exuded this same genuineness to them, a virtue that was undervalued in Nam. I guessed empathy was as essential to his job as machismo had been to ours.

My two new acquaintances gave the Chaplain and me the opportunity to repeat for everyone's benefit how we knew one another. It was interesting to hear the Chaplain's version of how, early in my tour, I had been assigned to help him repaint the shrapnel-ridden wooden shelter that served as a chapel on the base.

"When J.M. told me he had studied architecture before enlisting," he began, "I asked him to design amphitheater seating for the chapel and direct a construction crew."

"My first commission," I piped in.

"Well, you did a good job on the drawings, but why did you abandon management of the construction crew?" he asked, half complimentary and half playfully. He knew the answer.

"Well," I retorted a little defensively, "there was this little operation I had to go on for nearly three weeks."

"Yeah, I heard about that one. Operation Durham Peak in the Que Son Mountains," he replied knowingly. "We lost a lot of good men on that operation."

"We also kicked some ass," I added.

He turned to the other two Marines, our little audience, and continued his ribbing. "When he told me he spent four years in a Catholic seminary before Vietnam, I thought he could be trusted to follow through on his promises."

I was pleased he remembered this about me. My seminary experience was a bridge that helped us connect. He was the only officer who ever took a moment to get to know me, but I chafed a little at his disclosure. It was not something I casually revealed about myself. Although I was comfortable with the label "Catholic" imprinted on my dog tags when the Chaplain and I first met, I had rejected my faith completely by the time my tour ended.

"Did you ever find a replacement assistant?" I asked.

"I did," he answered, "but I would have preferred you."

"You know, I really thought about it when you first offered it. I thought it would be good duty until you found me in the bush that day last summer. Remember?"

"Yeah, I remember," said the Chaplain, his face scrunched down into a look of somber concern. "When I told you about my assistant...you remember him, don't you? Jeff Edwards. Short, skinny kid just out of high school, from Sacramento?"

"Vaguely," I replied, "only met him one time."

"Well, you looked a little shaken up when I told you Edwards got killed by a sniper. You cooled to the idea then..." the chaplain's voice trailed off into an uncomfortable moment of silence before I replied.

"Right. You and your assistant had the Bible and a prayer while I went around armed with a heavy mortar and surrounded by rifle company grunts. That seemed safer than working for you."

"The devil you know is better than the one you don't?" he said, as his smile returned to his face.

The Chaplain turned to the other two Marines, neither of whom had said a word so far, and continued, "As I recall, he was cooking some concoction over a campfire in a helmet."

"Yeah. It was peach cobbler. I'll have you know, I have quite the reputation as a C-rat cook," I boasted. "My parting gift to my unit three days ago was my cigar box of seasonings. Got to have that Red Sauce handy to make them edible."

"I'll bet," he countered, "But the cobbler was very good. Say, that gives me an idea. You guys be ready at sixteen hundred and I'll have a little surprise for you. Sound good?" We all agreed in unison. We had no alternative plans.

That afternoon, the three of us heard a jeep's beep. While squeezing into the Chaplain's vehicle, he offered only an obscure explanation, "We're going to celebrate our survival." We drove a short way and he pulled into a long driveway flanked by palm trees and manicured lawns and past a meticulously painted sign that read "Officer's Club." We knew those two words were also code for, "No Enlisted Personnel Allowed." Disregarding the prohibition, Capt. Hanson boldly led his miniature patrol through the two glass-paneled entry doors, past the elegantly appointed restaurant that was beginning to fill with officers in full uniform, and directly to the bar and its Oriental bar tender. The place was nearly full.

In a voice loud enough for all present to hear, he declared, "These Marines just got out of combat duty in Vietnam. They have done their duty and served their country. Give them whatever they want." I downed my cold beer with pride and actually enjoyed the stares from the officers.

Like a man with a mission, Chaplain Hanson then drove us off the Marine Corps base to an Oriental restaurant for a meal more rich in food and drink than I felt anyone deserved. We joined several others and sat cross-legged at a large table with a grill in its center. The Oriental chef stood in a shallow pit on the opposite side and performed food art. With the speed of a boxer and the skill of a pianist, he diced, sliced, skewered, and simmered our feast as we sat transfixed, engulfed in the aromas, and salivating.

Satiated, the good chaplain had even more in store for us. He drove to an unobtrusive white building set back from the road and led the way into an immaculate white lobby staffed by a demure Asian woman. He moved with such confidence, I sensed he'd done this before. After whispering instructions and handing over some bills, another woman appeared and steered us toward a large hot tub and left. Quickly, we peeled off our uniforms and exposed four deeply tanned bodies with butts as white as the walls. The water and heat penetrated deeply. At first we joked and drank Japanese beers. Over time, though, a quietness enveloped us with the steam. We were as contented as cows in Calcutta.

After showers, four beautiful Asian women arrived to offer us towels and guide us individually into small private rooms, each with a massage table in the center. Dazzled by this new experience, I innocently obeyed the gestures of the woman and laid face down on the table.

I don't remember her face. A downy white towel wrapped around her dark, lithe body. For a long time nothing happened. She busied herself out of view at a small table in the corner. Neither of us spoke. I sensed her approach. She removed my towel and began applying massage oils first to my shoulders with firm, smooth strokes. It was the first gentleness I'd experienced in eighteen months. With eyes closed and kinesthetic senses fully engaged, I ran a mental movie of the two of us. Only this movie had a blend of aromas and sensations: flowers, warmth, relief, smoothness, comfort, tenderness and the scent and feel of a woman's hands. As she massaged my arms and hands, legs and feet, ears, neck, lower back, and thighs, I sank deeper and deeper into a womb-like cocoon.

Slowly, she began to explore private areas by increasing the radius of each stroke. Probably sensing my embarrassment, she offered in a high-pitched, sing-song accent to keep going for "five dolla.'" Before my lolled brain could make a decision, she brought my wallet near my face and removed it from its protective plastic baggie releasing the smell and memory of Vietnam with it. In the process of rolling over onto my back, I removed the bill for her. Like plugging a short-term parking meter, I had to periodically feed her five dollar bills to get complete satisfaction. She was my first and only prostitute.

Afterwards, I thought how ironic that Father Schmidt condemned Bridget and me to Hell for making love, and Chaplain Hanson paid for me to have sex after going through hell.

15

Homecoming: Cleveland, Ohio; April 1970

...we may perceive positive qualities in people without empirical evidence to support such perceptions. This often happens in romantic encounters....Lovers, caught up in their desire for the other person, often project their own unconscious positive [shadow] attributes onto that person....When one is once "hooked" by a positive quality in another person, one may project all sorts of other positive qualities onto that person. This...is known as the "halo effect."

—Dr. William A. Miller, *Finding the Shadow in Daily Life*

The ink had hardly dried on my active duty discharge papers when I found myself in Dress Greens one last time and on a jet leaving San Diego bound for Cleveland. I was in uniform to qualify for the reduced military-standby rate, not because I felt comfortable wearing it among civilians. My mind was in a nether world; caught somewhere between the war zone I had left less than three weeks earlier, and the memory of normal life in the World. By the time I landed at Cleveland Hopkins International Airport, I was so anxious about meeting my family I could not bring myself to call for a ride to their home, only a few miles away. I had not even called to let them know I was coming.

After sitting on a bench in the airport lobby for over an hour, I called my older sister, Lynn, who lived in her own apartment nearby. She said she'd come but was completely befuddled why I would make her promise not to call our parents. The reunion with my sister was a mix of hugs and kisses, a flurry of questions, and Lynn's news that she was to be married in a few days. She didn't mention that none of the family members would be attending the ceremony because Mom and Dad disapproved of her choice of mate. She pulled rank on me and nixed my idea of either sneaking home late or going back to her place for the night so I could muster the courage to face the rest of my family the next morning.

We sat down and I confessed how guilty I felt for rarely writing my family while I was in Vietnam. I told her how Mom wrote regularly and how Dad added comments to most of the letters. Even my younger sister and four brothers added letters of their own. I tried to explain my survival technique of cutting myself off mentally from all things but the war. It was difficult to explain while refraining from any description of what the experience was really like. She must have understood it as a taboo topic because neither of us spoke the word "Vietnam." That conversation began a ten-year practice of evading that mine field. She handed me a dime and insisted I call home.

Mom was the first to welcome me at the front door. Her wiry arms entwined my waist and she bathed my face in kisses and tears. "Thank you, Jesus. Thank God, you're home. I let that seminary take my baby away from me and then that horrible war. Nothing else is going to take you away from me ever again." Her tears were a baptism of reclamation.

There was no judgment for the letters I never sent; no guilt for withholding any news about what had really happened over there; no condemnation for the concern I rarely felt and even less frequently expressed; no shame for my cowardice; no scorn for my participation in a scorned war; no insults for the bodies I left behind. I found only unquestioning love and acceptance.

I was home.

After Dad and the rest of the family went to bed, Mom and I sat around the dining room table for a while. She brought me up to date on all the family news, including their prohibition against attending my sister, Lynn's, wedding. Later, Mom walked me up to my brother, Denny's, room, vacant because he was studying journalism at Kent State University, and handed me a thick crumpled letter that bore tattered scars from rough handling.

"This came for you today."

I traced its past itinerary through the sequence of military stamps that began with the FPO (Fleet Post Office) First Marine Division Headquarters at Camp Pendleton, California; FPO I CORPS, 1st Mar. Div., Da Nang; the California address again, and lastly my parent's address in Cleveland. Bridget's return address in Kent, where she was still attending the University, rippled through the dimpled upper left corner.

"It's very late so I'll say good night now, Michael. It's good to have you home safe." Mom's warm smile melted into the hint of a frown. "I hope that girl's not going to be a problem." We exchanged hugs that were a little less warm, and she went to bed.

I drew the envelope to my nose just as I had done with every one of Bridget's letters. That same potpourri of perfume and the odors of Vietnam were my transport back to the fleeting sensation of serenity her letters offered me while I was in Nam. The femininity of her stationery, penmanship, and words formed a bubble around me that kept the war outside and the promise of a peaceful loving future inside. While some of the men in my unit turned to the Bible as an amulet to ward off fear, I turned to the baggie I always carried with my favorite letters from Bridget.

Before I opened her letter, I flashed back to the memory of the last time I saw Bridget before I left for Vietnam. In mid-March 1969, I was at Camp Pendleton killing time while awaiting orders. When told I might not leave for two weeks, I called Bridget and asked her to come out for an extended visit. She did and rented a little dive of a room for a week in Oceanside, California a few miles from the base. Two nights after she arrived I got an overnight pass. Along with the pass, I got my orders to ship out to Da Nang the next afternoon. I remember two things about this last good-bye—last lovemaking and last words.

Marine training builds incredible endurance and boundless horniness. Behind us were the rigors of training and its ability to displace with physical exhaustion the testosterone-driven urges of young men. Ahead of us loomed the uncertainty of combat in a strange land on the dark side of the planet. We were stuck in doldrums of inaction, the eye of a sexual tension hurricane.

I brought the building storm with me to that little room in Oceanside. The electricity of anticipatory nervous energy triggered the tightening of the tiny muscles at the base of my every hair follicle. Our first words were tentative and carefully chosen. Within a short time, we switched to the language in which we were most fluent. Our bodies reveled in their mother tongues as if they could be struck mute at any moment. It was a long conversation, sometimes heated, sometimes just silly with small talk, sometimes punctuated by words and cries that were indistinguishable from those born of anger and pain. We explored the limits of each other throughout that last long night.

With the rising of the sun and too few hours of sleep, we awoke totally spent and thus free to cleave the relationship that we had built over the prior eighteen months. We were free to sever the fragile graft that society and my parents helped husband. We were free to acknowledge the ax blade that would allow us to grow our separate ways. It was Bridget who named it and the naming brought it alive. "…and if you go over there to that hell-hole and get yourself fucked up…well, damn it…well, just fuck you for doing this. Fuck you and your Marine Corps and your need to prove yourself. That's it. Good-bye. Now get out."

I couldn't articulate my reasons for enlisting. I didn't know at the time my reasons. Language and inexperience failed me. I figured she'd get over it.

I hadn't heard from her at all during the last five weeks during which I both nurtured and was plagued by a sense of doom. In desperation deep in my underground bunker, I had broken my own prohibitions against fantasizing about the future and staged mental dramas of a romantic reunion. I played the part of the returning war hero and she the faithful and adoring lover. Still, no word came from the woman I had crowned as my queen and savior, no response to my frequent proclamations of everlasting love and subjugation. There was no reply, until now.

The raised voices of my parents from their bedroom down the hall brought me out of my reverie. My left ear, undamaged by mortars and incoming rounds, pricked at the name "Bridget" several times. They never forgave the woman who "stole" their son's virginity. Still standing transfixed in the middle of my younger brother's room with the weighty letter still unopened in my hands, I tore open the envelope and found two letters inside. The first was one of the last ones I wrote to Bridget from Vietnam and the second was a new one from her. Here's mine:

Dear Bridget,

I really have so much to tell you. I just lack the environment and ability to do it.

Your letter was a sunny day during the monsoons. Constant writing couldn't express the countless inexpressible thoughts of love I have for you. Bridget, you are unique in a way you don't even know. (Thinking about it—in quite a few ways....) And this uniqueness makes me unique. I'm the only one here I know that hasn't received a "Dear John" type letter at some time from his girl. Few married men here can match my trust and confidence—none to my credit, but you. We continue to match each other's love, despite all circumstances.

God! I'm tired of needing fading memories to make conscious that real but buried love—and the fear of doing it because of the resulting pain. I want you. I want to learn the meaning of words like: girl, love, kiss, blonde, Bridget. You're a stranger that I know better than anyone else in the world.

Sorry if I'm crying in my beer—just tired. I'm sure you are too—probably more so. Let my love help you.

Everybody that got here when I did leaves tomorrow. This Machine fucked up and scratched my name off the float list. I might leave on a slow boat in a few days or a few weeks, or a jet in a month or so.

Please write. All my love,
Michael

Her response was typed on regular bond paper, no flowery stationary or penmanship, no perfume:

Michael,

I don't know how to ease into this so I'll just come out and say it. I am so very sorry but this is not going to work out. I've been so afraid of writing this to you because I fear its effect on you, you being in a combat zone. But I have to be honest. You have to stop sending me these love letters. You have to stop loving me. It's over.

I never wanted you to go off to this stupid war. I'm not alone thinking this way. There's not a single one of your friends that support it. I hated that you went into the military and I hate the war even more because of that. I can't stand the idea of what you're doing over there and I have little sympathy for problems that resulted from your decision to go over there. You wouldn't listen to me or any of your friends. You were so God damn stubborn. You said you had to go and do your thing even though it meant we had to wait. Well, now I have something I need to do alone. And it won't wait for you.

Don't come looking for me. I do not want to see you. It's over.

Bridget

No signature.

The trouble with illusions is that you aren't aware of them until they are taken away from you. I decided after reading her second sentence to hitchhike the sixty miles to Kent first thing the next morning. When I arrived at the rundown rooming house, her rusty red, 1966 Corvair was parked in the drive but no one answered my knocks and shouts at the front door. The door was unlocked so I entered and began a search for her room. Like a voyeur, I peeped through the big keyhole on the door to the first bedroom I found and saw her sitting on the bed, head in hands, golden hair like a flag at half mast. This door was locked, and she was not about to unlock it no matter how urgent my pleas. With a kick that carried a year's worth of longing, the door yielded and I entered. When she looked up, her long hair could no longer hide her very pregnant belly. I read shame, anger, and utter disappointment in her downcast eyes. She probably read the same in mine. My knees went wobbly as I watched my fantasy reunion scene crash into reality. Deflated, I sat down next to her on the bed and she burst into tears again. My longing for her even overwhelmed the unanswered question posed by her condition. I hushed her faltering attempt at explanation and drew her down on to the bed in my arms where my tears mingled with hers. I was determined to play out at least some of my reunion fantasy.

Eventually, she told me about an innocent visit from an old boyfriend that led to too much laughter and too much drink. Her story ended with date rape and the transformation of the main character. Of course, I believed the story. I had too much at stake not to. She repeated the sentiment expressed in her letter, that her need to deal with this matter on her own was little different than my need to go off to war. We made no plans and I left her to visit my old college roommate, Jim, at Kent State.

I figured Bridget would resolve things her own way, alone.

16

A Retreat To Sea: The Great Lakes; April 1970

The war in Vietnam was without evident purpose for those who fought in it, and the return home was the very opposite of a hero's welcome. In consequence, the process of meaningful transformation was aborted, and many soldiers were left with psychic injury without any hope of healing or growth.

—Daryl S. Paulson, Ph.D., *Walking the Point*

"So, Son, what are your plans now that you completed your military service duty?" My dad's question four days after coming home from Vietnam didn't surprise me. He was a decisive man of action who abhorred wasting time. I told him I wasn't ready to return to school.

"I've been thinking about working on the ore boats, Dad." I had been fascinated since he took me as a young boy to the Cleveland docks on Lake Erie to see the ships that hailed from around the world. It must have struck him as odd that his son would come home after more than a year away and immediately think about leaving again. He didn't dismiss it outright, though. I'm sure he knew I was having girlfriend problems. I had told Mom the basics about Bridget's situation and I'm sure she told Dad. I suspected that Mom was delighted to hear the news because it verified her opinion of Bridget, but she didn't let on with me.

After my father died, I found a clew to his thinking at the time. He had saved one letter from me, the one that I recall addressing specifically to him about a month after I arrived in Vietnam. It reads, in part, "You're really the only one I could tell it 'like it is.' Who else can I share the feeling of seeing a fellow Marine twenty feet away knocked off his feet and twitching on the ground after catching an AK-47 round in the back of the head." Maybe Dad sensed a retreat at sea would do me some good.

I couldn't have been very pleasant to be around at the time. I was jumpy and my nervousness was contagious. I couldn't shake the memory of the architecture student who replaced me as my friend, Jim's, roommate and his opening question: "Did you have to kill women and children over there?" He delivered the line with an air of sanitized concern mixed with sarcasm. I could have given him an honest "yes" answer and then beat him to a pulp, or silently ignored him. I chose the latter. The accusation smoldered in me. Rather than bring up the War and risk disturbing me, my friends limited their conversations to the three "Cs:" cars, clothes, and chicks. I had left a place where I had responsibilities and a dangerous mission and then went home to people with whom I couldn't share my experiences. Instead, people wanted me to rejoin society as if nothing had happened over the past year. I was the alien in a society of strange values. After I assured Dad I would resume my architecture classes in the fall, he said he'd make a few calls to people he knew and see what he could do.

"You know, Son, during my month-long trip home by ship from Guam after the War, I dreamed up my plan to start my own company publishing suburban telephone directories." I had heard the story many times before how Dad foresaw the population explosion and the burgeoning of the suburbs after the soldiers came home. He figured people would want smaller local phone books and the businesses that would spring up in the suburbs would not want to pay high rates to advertise in the three-inch thick Cleveland phone book. He did build that successful business, Orange Line Publishing Company. It was many years later before I realized how the slow trip home from the Second World War helped Dad make the transition from soldier back to businessman. He must have sensed my need for the same retreat. Through his numerous contacts, my father secured a deckhand position for me at a time when the waiting list at the International Port of Cleveland for a Merchant Marine job was nine months to a year. He had that kind of influence. Two weeks later he dropped me off at the dock alongside the U.S. Steel iron ore carrier, *D. M. Clemson.*

Empty of cargo, she sat high in the water. The gleaming white pilot house towered the equivalent of six stories above me, and her auburn-colored hull filled everywhere my eyes could see. Thousands of rivets, each bearing the fingerprint of the riveter's gun, melded her 5-foot by 10-foot, half-inch thick steel plates into a graceful curve that carried her lines over 610 feet toward the mist-shrouded stern. A thin curl of black smoke spiraled out of the stack from the 2,000 horsepower steam boilers. I sensed this was the right thing to do. Within the hour, I sailed off toward Duluth, changing from Marine to Merchant Marine in a few short weeks.

I found the men of the *Clemson* to be as hardened as the steamship they sailed. They were an odd collection of solitary men with standoffish grimaces, men who were quick to laugh and slow to criticize, strong men tempered by the elements, women-hating men, men who missed their wives and families, and veterans from the country's three most recent wars. I fit right in.

Captain Brotz, the "Old Man," was one of the more interesting people aboard. For me he embodied one of the seafaring characters I had envisioned in the Horatio Hornblower novels I devoured as a kid. His many years serving on all types of vessels and on all kinds of seas crippled his legs and back terribly with rheumatism and arthritis. The Bosuns Mate said the Old Man used to stand over six feet tall and had a booming voice that automatically commanded respect. What I saw was a shriveled little man, twisted to the left from his shoulders to his knees. His bent back forced him to crane his neck just to see forward. As if hobbled between left foot and right shoulder, a step with his left foot jerked his right shoulder to the left, and the drag of his right foot re-cocked him for the next step. He moved with shear force by throwing his weight forward and then recovering to avoid falling on his face. Arms clutched his torso for stability, head fused to shoulders. To watch his slow tortured walk evoked fascination, sympathy, embarrassment, and thankfulness for health.

Two days out of port, a 360-degree view from the *Clemson's* deck revealed the gray-blue ice of a completely frozen Lake Michigan. The scene was devoid of shorelines and features other than the deep blue wake cut by the 290-foot Coast Guard icebreaker, the *Mackinaw*, which steamed directly ahead of us. We were the first ore carrier out that year. I shivered constantly in my new world. It was a hundred degrees colder than the one I had left a month earlier. I knew comforting warmth only when I could hide under a wool cocoon of blankets at night.

Not all nights were cozy, however. About a month into the job, I awoke to the timeless cry of nautical alarm.

"All hands on deck!"

My emergency reactions still honed, I was out of my bunk and throwing on clothes before I became fully cognizant of the high-pitched whine of the wind. It screamed counterpoint to the pained sounds of heavy-gauge steel straining to its limits. The cabin pitched about madly. In the low light, I spotted little streamlets trickling down the stairs.

The deck watch, Red, burst into the cabin repeating the order. "Those are gale-force winds out there and it's Lake Superior, so dress for it!"

I bunked with the two other deckhands. Wendell, a dimwitted kid who seemed to have learned nothing from his year as a supply clerk at an Army post near the Mekong Delta, was nearly impossible to wake. I left that task to the other deckhand, Frank, a fellow college student from Kent State.

I was the first of us to emerge from the crew quarters hatch and beyond the protective overhang. The wind lashed my face with an arsenal of icy water pellets and choked me with its ferocity. Over the sound of the wire flagstaff stays screaming in the blast like the strings a tortured violin, I heard Red bellow at the top of his lungs, "Batten down the hatches!" I struggled toward the ship's starboard rail to fetch a handful of the steel clamps and tried in vain to snap the top of my rain coat. The *Clemson* pitched dangerously to starboard. I grabbed for the rail as a sheet of near-freezing Lake Superior water tugged at my rubber boots.

As my eyes adjusted to the sickly yellow-green, pre-dawn light that squeezed between roiling thunderheads, I set more clamps to secure the massive hatch covers to the hatch walls. Soon, my two deck mates and the Bosuns Mate joined Red and me in the task. The First Mate arrived and took a lookout position amidships, his head craned into the onslaught.

The urgency of the moment quickly cleared my head. I'd had only a couple hours of sleep after an all-night shift loading the ship in Duluth with Minnesota's Mesabi Range taconite. As the brain sharpened, the body dulled. Bone weariness hastened the stiffening chill that crept from my fingertips and up through each digit as I tried to snag the hook end of the big clamp to the eyelet on the hatch wall, guide the screw end through the hatch cover bracket, and tighten the huge wing nut with the waning strength of my wrist and fingers. I cursed for not having grabbed my thick rubber gloves.

A moment later, the First Mate screamed over the howl of the gale **"Run to port!"**

Although the order made no sense to me, I found myself half sailing on the wind, half sliding on the wet deck toward the down sloping port rail before I finished questioning the order. Military training runs deep. A massive arm of Lake Superior water, black and bespewed with foaming white splotches, came at us over the starboard side like a big wet fist. Like trapeze artists, we clung to that bar of steel while the wave pitched the ship madly to port once again and then tried to upend her as if she were made of cork instead heavy plate steel. The churning cataract broke angrily and swept the deck.

With more clamps in hand, we returned to our tasks. The seas kept building and the cycle repeated several times until it became more of a thrilling game. Could we complete the job before our frozen fingers gave out, or would the lake wear us down, then swallow us whole? Being swept overboard meant death from hypothermia in less than twenty minutes—if you could stay afloat, five if you didn't. I wondered if the coverage in my ten thousand dollar military life insurance policy would extend to the Merchant Marines.

Suddenly, the simultaneous explosion of thunder and lightening burned an unforgettable scene into my eyes. In the battle between the forces of water and wind, a towering wall of dark blue-black water, iced by a gossamer veil of gray foam and topped by delicate sprays, formed the backdrop off the stern to starboard. The impossible was happening. The bow, one hundred feet forward of my position, had just crested a mountainous wave and was cutting through it on an extreme angle while the ship's rudder, five hundred feet to my rear, was still trapped in the trough of the same wave. The *Clemson*, sailing downwind, formed the diagonal of a "Z" with the top and base of the letter representing the tremendous wave crests.

The thought of being totally engulfed made me queasy. I watched transfixed, temporarily in awe as the front slope of water began to overtake and raise the stern. The next lightning strobe exposed its gray marbly skin, like bad meat, and the hundreds of ghostly tendrils that arched off its crest. It broke ten feet higher than the stern's second deck, a full twenty feet higher than the main deck where we were frantically working.

Somehow, I caught the broken order of the First Mate: "**Get... Center...atches!**"

Another flash of lightning revealed the fractured wave scouring its way between the hatches in search of something to steal before it was spent. By the time the avalanching water reached the hatch I had climbed up on, it still had the power to surge two feet of water like a Class V rapids over the deck and through the gunwale ports.

Our next task was to string a cable down the center of the ship from fore to aft to serve as a safety line. With the task accomplished, we huddled in the galley where the cook kept a twenty-four-hour supply of steaming coffee and warm, fresh donuts.

As we reheated our bodies, the Old Man paid us a visit to congratulate us on a job well done. He said that had we not been carrying a load of taconite, that wave might have capsized and sunk the ship. I discovered later that it would have been the second *D. M. Clemson* to be lost on Lake Superior. The first *Clemson* was last seen at 9:30 a.m. on Sunday, December 1, 1908, bound for Duluth with six thousand tons of ore. She is unreported to this day.

Replenished by the middle-of-the-night break, we headed back to our forward crew quarters. The mad pitching of the ship made the trip difficult as we clung to the lifeline and clambered up and down over each of the hatches. Amidships, the lights on the rail revealed a bowed and deformed little man lurching his way along the yawing and rolling deck. I paused and tightened my grip on the cable to steady myself in this world where nothing would stand still. It was the Old Man, navigating that reeling deck without the slightest variation of his jerking gate. Without as much as a handhold on the rail, he walked a line as straight and methodical as he would in port.

I thought of how Vietnam left me with a psychic limp. I was anxious for the time when I would again be able to face life's storms and walk a straight line in spite of that limp.

As my days on the *Clemson* began to melt into each other with the predictability of the ship's regimen, I came to realize that I had instinctively wanted to sequester myself from the very world I had so desperately craved while in Vietnam. The four months I spent aboard ship among my fellow misfits and castaways provided that incubation period. It was a closed society that offered a safety zone where I could decompress before I fully reentered civilization. I remembered my dad's stories about his slow trip home by ship after the Second World

War and how the soldiers discussed their experiences with one another. He saw how the men helped one another come to grips with their experiences. The ship was a safe place for them. He had found a ship and made it safer for me.

17

The War At Home: Kent State University; May 1970

One always learns one's mystery at the expense of one's innocence.

—Robertson Davies

The timing was perfect. On May 1, 1970, the *D.M. Clemson* docked for three days of repairs at her home port in Conneaute, Ohio, a steel town east of Cleveland near the Pennsylvania border. This was the very day Bridget was scheduled to give birth to her child at a Catholic hospital in Akron. I told my deckmates about my plan and thumbed the 140 miles to the hospital by way of Cleveland. By the time I arrived late that evening, Bridget's child had already come into the world and had been assigned adoptive parents through Catholic Charities. It was May Day and Bridget's twenty-second birthday. We had the briefest of visits, almost cordial. She had seen the thing through her way, alone.

Afterwards, I hitched the twenty miles to Kent to crash at the apartment of my former architecture classmate, Jim. I hardly spoke with the man who gave me the lift from the hospital. Maybe he could sense my melancholy over Bridget. At about midnight, he dropped me a few blocks from North Water Street, close to the string of bars just north of Main Street in downtown Kent.

One of the town's little black squirrels peered at me from its perch in the crotch of a towering elm as I watched through different eyes the town that had been home during two years at college before my enlistment. It wasn't just me that had changed. On that warm Friday night, instead of hearing the rocking tunes of the James Gang and the Numbers Band blaring from the Ron-De-Vu and the Kove, I heard loud voices and the crack and tinkle of plate glass breaking from the front of Thompson's Drugstore. Hundreds of people milled about. Motorcyclists of the Cobras gang from Youngstown and the local Chosen Few gang congregated according to their "colors" astride their throaty choppers. Twinkling lights, reflected by the shards of glass from smashed shop windows, created a theatrical backdrop for the drunken revelers who danced around flaming trash barrels. The scene brought to mind the race riot I witnessed in Cleveland's Hough District in 1967, but it felt more festive and exuberant than dangerous.

When I heard the oncoming wail of police sirens, I headed off toward Main Street and my friend's apartment via a side street and past the Haunted House that served as the model for Hitchcock's movie "Psycho." As I came down the hill towards Main, I saw police organizing for riot control. I flanked them and came upon a cluster of thirty or so students milling about at Main and Lincoln Streets. Some students climbed the light poles and the low brick walls of Prentice Gate, presumably to get a better view of the police activities. A few started a chant, "Pigs off campus! Pigs off campus!" It didn't catch on. Someone threw something down the street at the cops. Since the cops were way out of range for even the best pitching arm, the effect was more symbolic than militant.

I approached one kid who looked too young to be a college student and asked what was happening. He gave me a biting reply, "Where the hell you been, man? Mars? You didn't hear about Nixon's speech yesterday? He admitted that he invaded Cambodia." He didn't wait for a reply and instead proceeded to illuminate my ignorance. "First he wins the election on the campaign promise that he has a plan to end the War, and instead he expands it to a neutral country." Later I learned that on-campus antiwar protests had been heating up all day since the news. There had been a lot more attention back home to the War than I was aware of while fighting it.

It was some time later that I made it to my friend, Jim's, apartment and heard his assessment. "Politics and protests? Bull! This is the first warm spring night we've had. Kids are just blowing off steam before finals. The cops completely over-reacted." I told him people broke windows, spray-painted antiwar slogans on storefronts, and trashed the streets. "I was there, too, just trying to listen to my friend, Phil Keaggie, and the Glass Harp band at J.B.'s," he countered. "If the cops hadn't closed all the bars and forced us all out on the street, it would have just blown over. I was lucky I didn't get arrested for just being in the wrong place at the wrong time." Jim and I then focused more on the turmoil in our personal lives, especially mine.

Early the next evening, Saturday, May 2, I hitched back to the hospital for another visit with Bridget. I told her what I observed at Kent, but she was only interested in putting her pregnancy, the adoption, and me behind her. After about twenty minutes, she asked me to leave. Her voice was even, her stare resolute. When she turned in her hospital bed away from me, I left, dismissed. Like Classical Greek sculpture, she was detached, formal, and stoic.

I couldn't take my mind off Bridget. In her eyes, the War cut us apart. In mine, the War welded my fantasy for Bridget with my life-and-death experiences. That fantasy burned like shrapnel in my heart.

Late that night on the way back to Kent, the man who gave me a ride asked why I would want to go there. "Those outside agitators are stirring things up again. That campus is a hotbed. There's bound to be street action and trouble." After he dropped me off, I walked toward that same intersection of Lincoln and Main where I had seen the protests the night before. A group of about eighty people clustered on the south side of the intersection near the main entrance to the campus. I needed a distraction from planning how to win back Bridget. I got the distraction, an armored personnel carrier. Like a massive green beetle, the M113 Armored Cavalry Assault Vehicle from the 107 Armored Cavalry Regiment squeaked and rumbled up Main Street toward the campus. A helmeted Ohio National Guardsman sat atop its turret, manning the .30 Cal. machine gun. He had his weapon readied with a live ammunition belt that trailed from the breach. The gunner had the same power-crazed look I had seen so often just a few months earlier in Vietnam.

Now I sensed real danger. A unit of about thirty Guardsmen marched in a haphazard formation behind the tank. I thought their faces conveyed determination. I learned later it was probably fatigue because they had been pulled off crowd control duty for the Teamster's strike that crippled Akron and Cleveland. They carried their M1 rifles diagonally in front of them in the present-arms position with their ten-inch bayonets affixed to the barrels. Their rifles were standard issue throughout World War II so they were older than virtually every Guardsman who carried them. Oversized gas mask bags flopped at their left sides. The juxtaposition of college campus and tank troops was mind boggling. I thought I had left this insanity on the other side of the world. I thought of the campus as a sacrosanct place, a womb for learning. How had the War spread from the mosquito-infested jungles to my campus? Why had it followed me home?

A young woman standing to my left began to cry. "Why are they here? What are they doing on our campus?" she asked to nobody in particular as both her hands rose in supplication. A man who looked to be in his thirties answered her lament. "That's easy. We burned down the ROTC building tonight. The Governor called in the Guard to put down the riot." I looked in the direction of the dilapidated building that was used by the University's Reserve Officer's Training Unit, but the venerable old campus buildings and ancient elms blocked any view. I did notice the distinct scent of tear gas and the clear ring of the old Victory Bell coming from the direction of the Commons, the crossroads of the campus. Students had a long tradition of using this huge bell to rally others into the open green of the Commons. Located at the base of Blanket Hill, it was housed in a low ceremonial brick memorial dedicated to nothing in particular and accessible to all. Its clanging song carried messages such as, "We beat OU in football! Come to the Victory Rally, now!" "Free Bobby! Free Huey!" (referring to Seal and Newton, respectively). "I scored last night!" If I could have translated its message that night, I would have heard "Burn, baby, burn! Down with the military industrial complex! U.S. out of Cambodia! Pigs off campus! ROTC off campus!" As a student in 1968, I watched antiwar protesters use the bell to muster a crowd and then march the group to the opposite end of the Commons where the ROTC building, a former World War II barracks, served as the stage set for many an impassioned speech on peace. If I had answered the Victory Bell's clarion call that night of May 2, I could have seen the twenty-foot high flames that consumed Kent State's small, two-story, wooden symbol of America's military aggression.

Instead, I saw about eighty students lined up on the campus side of Main Street as if watching the annual Homecoming Parade. As the Guardsmen slowly marched up the street behind their bizarre "float" of a tank, the students shouted epithets at them and flashed them the finger. Someone started the chant, "One, two, three, four. We don't want your fucking war! Five, six, seven, eight. We won't live in a fascist state!" It died out after a few repetitions. A young woman began to scream obscenities, apparently for the sheer glory of being a part of something that was clearly momentous. A Huey chopper flew low overhead and I waited for the doorgunner to waste some peasants. Instead, it swept the street with its floodlight. Its loudspeaker boomed, "Disperse! This is an unlawful assembly. You must disperse immediately!" A TV news crew came on duty to further sensationalize the scene.

The presence of the National Guard on campus spooked me. I wanted nothing to do with the military ever again in my life. The crowd fell in at a distance behind the tank and its riflemen and the entourage progressed up the middle of Main toward the Prentice Gate entrance to the campus. Instead of following, I decided to check on my younger brother, Denny, who was a sophomore at Kent at the time. I tracked him down in his dormitory. He was wide awake with his girlfriend, Linda, and watching the TV news film of the events that had happened within sight of his dorm. The newscaster stated there had been two thousand antiwar protesters present and that the damage would total close to one hundred thousand dollars. He then rebroadcasted the spectacular footage of the ROTC building going up in flames and the arrival of the armored personnel carriers. The TV camera crew had failed to capture the dramatic difference in scale between the angry students who threatened with words and symbols, and the power and authority of the tank and soldiers. The scene on the little TV seemed so much smaller than what I had just witnessed an hour earlier. It was foreshortened as if the footage had been taken through the wrong end of a telephoto lens.

Later, we had one of our old familiar heart-to-heart talks about family, the War, school, girlfriends, and the riots. I told Denny about my mixed-up feelings. I never supported violent protests so I told him I understood the Mayor's decision to declare the city under a state of emergency and even the Governor's decision to call in the Guard after the destruction of government property. I could certainly sympathize with the plight of the Guardsmen. "The poor jerks," I said. "They probably joined the Guard to dodge the draft and a tour in Vietnam. Then the Governor calls 'em up to face down the antiwar protesters. Hell, the activists are blaming the Guard as the scapegoats even though they're probably classmates." Then, as usual, I flipped sides. "I also understand the protesters. I think most of them are out there because they believe in what they're doing." The confused attitudes I had about the War before enlisting were even more muddled after fighting in it.

"Hell, most of the protesters are out there because it's fun," opined my little brother. "When Linda and I heard there was going to be some action tonight, we hid a six-pack of Schlitz Malt Liquor in a DuBois Bookstore bag and went up to Blanket Hill to watch the show. First the students were by the Victory Bell, then they went over by the ROTC building."

"You were right there?" I asked.

"Sure. Saw the whole thing. Anyway, somebody used a flare to start the old rat trap on fire but the building wouldn't catch. Later, it started up again and then it really took off. Made a cool bonfire. Fantastic. People were dancing around it, waving flags, and screaming. It was a carnival, man. Then we heard all these popping sounds, like popcorn."

"Ammunition?" I guessed.

"Yea, lots of it. The Fire Department came and then the National Guard. The Guard yelled over a bullhorn to 'disperse,' and to 'clear the area.' The Fire Department put out the fire, the students dispersed, we ran out of beer and then staggered back here." He was matter-of-fact about it all, almost flippant. "Hey, it's been fun."

"If so, it's dangerous fun." I knew what the Guardsmen were capable of doing. I told Denny that, when stationed at Camp Pendleton after returning from Vietnam, my unit completed crowd control training. The 1st Marines had responsibilities for riot control in San Diego and other Southern California cities just like the National Guard had in Ohio.

Tactics hadn't changed since the ancient Greek phalanx. We donned flak jackets and helmets, clipped our bayonets onto the barrels of our M14 rifles, and pulled gas masks over our faces. Shoulder to shoulder, we formed up six wide and six deep on the parade grounds. On command, we took a half step with our left boot and stomped it down on the pavement, hard and loud. We followed with the right and progressed slowly forward twelve inches at a time, stomp by stomp. On another command, those of us in the front row snapped our rifles and bayonets from the present-arms position, to pointing them directly in front us from our right sides. With each step of the left boot, we thrust our bayonets forward and retrieved them with the movement of the right boot.

Perception changes when sight, sound, and smell are encased in a gas mask. Only tunnel vision through the foggy plastic goggles is possible; the ominous sound of ones own deep breathing fills the background; and the smells of sweat, rubber, and old tear gas permeate. The dominating perception is the sound and feel of thirty-six simultaneous crashes of leather combat boots against hard pavement. Our boots echoed among the surrounding buildings and they reverberated through all thirty-six of us. Anonymous in our masks of war, we could fire tear gas from our grenade launchers to burn the lungs of our enemies while we breathed that same poison with impunity. We were no longer thirty-six individuals personally liable for our actions. We were a single armored creature with thirty-six pairs of legs and eyes, and one brain that gave commands. We were fearless, motivated, unstoppable, and impregnable. A human tank.

"That's what those protesters might find themselves up against," I warned as I crashed for the night on the floor.

The next morning, Sunday, I tried to call Nic, another friend of mine. I knew his brother had served early on in the War. When I first got back home two months earlier and talked to him, he told me he had lost a close friend over there and that another friend was still a prisoner of war. I wanted to check in on Nic but he didn't answer my call to his apartment next to the Robin Hood restaurant on Main Street.

I said good-bye to my brother, Denny, urged him to be careful, and escaped the growing conflict on campus to visit my family in Cleveland. I had to catch my ship before she left home port in Conneaute. As I hitch-hiked home, I kept thinking of the stark contrast between the tremendous sense of power that riot training gave me, and the lame powerlessness I felt as a civilian facing the weapons instead of brandishing them. Without an escape to my ship and safe harbor, I would have had to choose sides again in the War. Rejoin the military side I just left, or the ranks of my fellow student protesters? I fled the choice.

That same Sunday, May 3, Ohio Governor James A. Rhodes, who was running in a heated reelection primary two days later, threw fuel on the fire. He described the recent events in Kent to the hungry press as "probably the most vicious form of campus-oriented violence yet perpetrated by dissident groups and their allies in the State of Ohio." He pledged to use "every form of law" to control them. He then drove onto the campus, which was by then completely occupied by his National Guardsmen, and yelled over a bullhorn that the antiwar protesters were "worse than the Brown Shirts, and the Communist element, and also the nightriders and vigilantes. They're the worst type we harbor in America," and he vowed to "eradicate them." President Nixon added his venom to the situation by calling the antiwar protesters "bums," and then-Governor Ronald Reagan of California added that, "if it takes a blood bath, let's get it over with. No more appeasement."

I heard none of this inflammatory rhetoric at my parents' home in Cleveland. I had a ship to catch, so early Monday morning, May 4, I left with head down and thumb pointed east. Conneaute was not an easy port to get to and I missed the *Clemson's* departure by less than an hour. However, the harbormaster suggested I go to Detroit, hitch a ride on the mail boat, and board my ship as she steamed up the Detroit River. I made it to Detroit by thumb and by bus early Tuesday morning, walked to the harbor area, and waited for an hour until the captain of the mail boat arrived. He agreed to take me aboard.

While I was chasing the *Clemson*, an event that would rock the world was happening on the campus I had just left. At 12:24 p.m. on Monday, May 4, twenty-eight Guardsmen fired sixty-seven rounds in thirteen seconds at a group of unarmed students. They wounded nine and killed four students: Bill Schroeder, Allison Krause, Sandy Sheuer, and Jeffrey Miller.

I knew none of this as I waited on that Detroit dock and sipped hot coffee with the captain of the mail boat. When the *Clemson* emerged from the early morning fog, we motored out to greet her. We matched her speed exactly, stayed about ten feet abeam, and rode in the trough created by her bow wave. My fellow deck mates hauled up the mail and newspapers and unrolled a rope ladder over the side after spotting me. My stomach fluttered some as I grasped for the umbilical to the mother ship and then swung out over the open water. I pondered my moves if I slipped or the ladder failed. Would I be sucked under and ground to hamburger by the *Clemson's* screws? Finding no answer, I started the slow, careful three-story climb up the side of the ship. The wind and ship's motion started a giant pendulum swing of my ladder parallel to the ship's great steel hull. With each step, the movement grew stronger and cycled faster.

I looked up to see my fellow crewman, Frank, holding up the just-delivered issue of the *Detroit Free Press*. Printed in four-inch type face was the headline: "FOUR DEAD IN OHIO." Below it was the picture that would symbolize the era, the end of the 60s, and the home theater of the Vietnam War. It was of Mary Ann Vecchio, a 13-year-old runaway from Opa Locha, Florida, on bent knee with arms outstretched and face upturned in a tortured look of despair. In front of her was the dead lump, missing the top of its head, that had been Jeff Miller. Impulsively, I started back down the ladder but saw there was no mail boat there to take me back to my campus.

I wanted to find out if my brother, Denny, and his girlfriend, Linda, were safe. I didn't know that they had hid behind a tree twenty feet from the Pagoda next to Taylor Hall where the National Guard troops turned and unleashed their firepower at the students.

"I thought the 'weekend warriors' were firing blanks," he told me later. "When I found out they shot the students—I saw all the people around the bodies on the ground—I went into a rage. Shock. Tear gas was stinging my eyes. I just wanted to kill them because they had killed us, but I grabbed Linda and got us the hell out of there."

I wanted to know if my friend, Jim, was safe. I didn't know that, after completing a final exam on Structural Analysis of Buildings in Taylor Hall, he walked out on the building's veranda just in time to see the Guard unit turn around on command and assume firing positions. He was twenty feet from the soldiers and forty from Denny and Linda when he when saw the Guardsmen open fire. Hiding behind the structure's towering columns, he heard the order to fire, heard all sixty-seven shots, and heard the screams thirteen seconds later to cease firing.

"I heard somebody say behind me, 'Hey, somebody's shooting off firecrackers.' I thought they were blanks," he told me later.

I wanted to know if my friend, Nic, was safe. I didn't know he had escaped the earlier sweep of that same Guard unit into the practice field in front of Taylor Hall by climbing over the fence at the edge of the field. He knew they weren't firing blanks because he heard the rounds go over his head. He saw their victims fall and the pools of blood form and run down the pavement in Taylor Hall's parking lot.

"My two friends and I were with Sandy Sheuer. She was a speech therapy student who didn't participate in any of the protests," he told me later. "She was simply walking to her next class in the Music and Speech building when she was hit. While someone gave her mouth-to-mouth, we tried to keep her neck together. There was so much blood. So much blood. After an ambulance finally took her away—I held the door for her stretcher—we went over to the spot where her friend, Jeff Miller, died. An ambulance had already taken away his body. Someone dipped a flag in the pool of his blood and kept waving it all around. At first I couldn't believe what I was seeing, then the anger set in. I could have killed a Guardsman, any Guardsman. I could have killed Nixon. I had so much anger. It was such a tragic misuse of power."

Those four days in May and thirteen seconds on May 4 charged the world with electricity. Mine was not the only campus to see a militaristic response to antiwar protest. Ten days later, twelve students were wounded and two killed at Jackson State University by repeated and wanton fusillades from Mississippi Highway Safety Patrolmen and Jackson City police. The Scranton Report, *Report of the President's Commission on Campus Unrest*, describes the ferocity of this attack on student protests. The officers used a submachine gun, shotguns, and rifles to fire more than 150 rounds into Alexander Hall where many of the students had fled for safety. The tragedy at Jackson State mixed antiwar protests with the racial hatred in America. All of the officers were white and all of the victims were black.

Four hundred colleges and universities went on strike or closed as a result of the shootings. The Scranton report summarized the Kent State tragedy: "The actions of some students were violent and criminal and those of some others were dangerous, reckless, and irresponsible. The indiscriminate firing of rifles into a crowd of students and the deaths that followed were unnecessary, unwarranted, and inexcusable." According to *Nam, the Vietnam Experience 1965-75*, a leaked FBI investigation concluded "the shootings were not necessary and not in order," and "we have some reason to believe that the claim by the National Guard that their lives were endangered by the students was fabricated subsequent to the event." Even so, when they were brought to trial the Guardsmen were all found not guilty. Eight and a half years later, the defendants signed a statement expressing regret and admitted responsibility for the shootings. On January 4, 1979, in an out-of-court settlement, the parents and students were awarded $675,000 from the State of Ohio.

The country was never more polarized than during this period. Few wept over the victims, especially the "silent majority," as President Nixon loved to call his supporters. Days after the shootings, the *Akron Beacon Journal* quoted Seabury Ford, a local leader and Chairman of the Republican Party in Portage County: "Why didn't the Guard shoot more of them?" It was not an isolated sentiment. People began using a gesture of four fingers up to mean, "The score is four, next time more." It was repeated often, even by parents of college students, even by Denny's and my parents.

It was a time in this country when practicing democracy could get one killed.

18

The Times They Are a Changing: June 1970

Cherish your doubts, for doubt is the attendant of truth....A belief which may not be questioned binds us to error, for there is incompleteness and imperfection in every belief. Doubt is the touchstone of truth; it is an acid that eats away the false....Those that would silence doubt are filled with fear....[Doubt] is to the wise as a staff to the blind; doubt is the attendant of truth.

—Robert T. Weston

It was a time of change with everything in motion. I lay in my bunk and listened to the soothing sounds of the *Clemson*. Her half-century-old metal moaned and creaked as she rode Lake Superior's waves at fifteen knots toward Duluth, where she was to take on fourteen thousand tons of taconite. I had not sailed long enough for my sense of balance to be one with the complex roll, yaw, and pitch of the ship. My life rolled, yawed, and pitched like the *Clemson*, and my personality reshaped itself in response to the wave action of my experiences. I saw little constancy during the five months since I left the relative safety of my bunker under the Second Section's hooch. As I tried to make the transition from soldier to citizen, I discovered someone had invaded my girlfriend's womb. My President's troops invaded the neutral country of Cambodia. My Governor's troops invaded my campus at Kent State and shot my classmates.

Although I could not predict Lake Superior's next motion, the rhythms of life aboard ship were reliably regular. The personalities of the *Clemson's* crew seemed riveted in place, but for me, it was time for a change.

Rather than grab a couple more hours of valuable sleep before the early morning mooring, I lay awake to contemplate my next move. One decision could chart a whole new course to a very different destination. I still harbored the vision that had sustained me in Vietnam of a future with Bridget. I called her from every port and found her sinking slowly into a morose sea of self-pity and blame. In Vietnam, we used to say the worst day in the World is better than the best day in the Nam, but her dark moods were making me question the adage. My elation at surviving wrestled with my survivor's guilt. I still clung tenuously to the hope she would grow to love me again, but my grasp was slipping. I heard a faint death rattle in our relationship.

The ship's bells indicated two a.m. I dropped the blinds over my memory of Bridget and drifted off to sleep with pleasant thoughts instead about Cynthia, the dear friend I had met at the top on the Empire State Building. With the sounding of the bells four hours later, the deck watch woke my other two deckmates with orders to prepare the *Clemson's* hatches for taking on taconite. Hot coffee and fresh donuts awaited us in the galley. I had made two decisions in those early morning hours lying in my bunk. I would quit my job after we loaded the ship, and I would hitch to St. Paul to visit Cynthia.

My next bed was a lumpy one in the soon-to-be condemned and demolished Andrews Hotel in Downtown Minneapolis. I waited for Cynthia to get off work so we could visit. There had been surprise but no hesitation in her voice when I called from Duluth earlier in the day with my plan to visit her. Two years and one lifetime had passed since we sat and talked on the Coney Island beach. During that time, we were on parallel courses but with different people, she with her husband and me with Bridget. We both invested in relationships with the hope that, some day, they would blossom and transform our lives. She had read and reread the letters I sent her from Vietnam but had to throw them away to protect her new marriage. We spent only a few hours together, but the brief meeting nurtured the seed that we had planted two years earlier in New York City. It would take another three years to bloom.

Those three years were filled with momentous changes. Cynthia saw her marriage through to the birth of Jessica in March 1972. She wrote to me that motherhood had changed her, made her fiercely protective. "Now I know what unconditional love is all about," she wrote. She said she refused to raise Jessica in the loveless place of her marriage. When even their therapist told them they needed divorce, not marriage counseling, they took her advice.

My three years apart from her were wild ones. Blind to the authenticity of what I shared with Cynthia, I was still determined to resuscitate the unrealistic relationship with Bridget that was so important to retaining my sanity in Vietnam. Seven months after reading her "Dear John" letter, I married Bridget. Our marriage ended a short nine months later. Our relationship had come full term. I was finally ready for the birth of my new life without Bridget.

In the two years between my separation from Bridget and the summer of 1973, I packed in a lot of living and worked a wide variety of jobs—press operator in an automotive plant, piano tuner, carpenter in New Orleans' French Quarter, foreman in a modular housing manufacturing plant, door-to-door salesman, and computer programmer. I also finished another year of college, participated in the antiwar movement, and immersed myself in the Hippie counter-culture that thrived at the University and the town of Kent.

In the summer of 1973, I came to Minnesota for a railroad construction job and moved in with Cynthia and Jessica. We gave ourselves the summer to decide whether we'd stay dear friends or commit to something more. I knew within three weeks I could spend my life with Cynthia, but this was a package deal. Husband was one thing; father to sixteen-month-old Jessica was quite another.

On Friday night, July 13, I came home after being away for a week on my job and found Jessica sitting in her highchair with a welcoming smile on her little face. Cynthia had dressed up and was ready to serve her special recipe for broccoli pie. We sat at the table together, the three of us, as Jessica smeared the pie all over herself and giggled impishly. My heart swelled, a father's heart. I had tried desperately to leave the War behind me and to resurrect what never was fully alive with Bridget. The acceptance of my failures awakened an epiphany of new possibilities. Were it not for Bridget, I could never fully appreciate the treasures I had before me. Were it not for Cynthia, the road back towards "normal" would have been much rockier. I proposed marriage to the two of them. We became a family. It was a time of change.

19

Leo: Cleveland, Ohio; September 1970

Vietnam was the most divisive time of battle in our country since the Civil War. It was the third most pivotal experience in this century—following the Depression and World War II. Its consequences are still being felt in our foreign policy, our troubled economy, in a haunted generation, in the new generation faced with possible new Vietnams, and in our hearts and minds. And yet because we lost, many refuse to face its monumental importance....

America lost its virginity in Vietnam. A protective cloak of morality and mysticism made defensible whatever was done in World War I, World War II and Korea.

—Myra MacPherson, *Long Time Passing*

As the soldier prays for peace, he must be prepared to cope with the hardships of war and bear its scars.

—General William C. Westmoreland, "Vietnam in Perspective"

Seven months after I left Vietnam, I had the urge to visit Leo, the only other Vietnam combat vet I knew from home. Leo and I attended high school together at Borromeo Seminary, back when we both thought we had a calling to become Catholic priests. By our senior year, secular voices and loud hormonal urges overcame the *sotto voce* of vocation that had originally lured us to the seminary. Our friendship solidified as we distanced ourselves from the clique of seminarians who were more certain of their calling, and then later discovered we had both joined the Marines after a couple of years of college.

Under a clear blue sky brushed with cirrus clouds, the towering elms and oaks created a living cathedral that embraced Cleveland's Lake Street. The trees wore a natural plumage that fall morning that mocked the artificial orange paint of my brand new 1970 VW bug. I had the convertible top down on my way to Leo's parent's house and relished the freedom to breathe in the trees as they rusted into their fall colors, their last act of spectral independence before a winter hibernation.

I didn't even know if Leo lived there anymore. He would have left Vietnam a year before that day and might be living anywhere. But I didn't want to spoil my surprise by calling his parent's home to find out if he was there, and risk tipping him off. It didn't matter. The chance that I could spring a surprise visit on him was worth the risk of a wasted drive from Kent on that beautiful Saturday morning. I owed him a surprise visit.

It was under very different circumstances almost a year and a half earlier that Leo paid a surprise visit to me. Marine Cpl. Leo Heath found out where I was stationed and hitched rides through sixty miles of Vietnamese countryside to get to my outpost. On a base with over two hundred men, he found me cleaning my rifle outside my hooch. I instantly recognized him, although he was a good thirty pounds leaner than when I saw him last. His broad face, blonde crew-cut hair, laughing eyes, and wide, crooked smile were unmistakable. High school memories flooded back as he gave me a bear hug and we executed a six-stage handshake. I didn't know then the exact location of my first fire support base, nor had I ventured off it since arriving. For

Leo to figure out my whereabouts and then walk most of the way there through a combat zone was to me the equivalent of walking on water. Leo was a welcome apparition.

Unfortunately, it had taken him so long to find me, we only had a short time to reminisce about our seminary years. I don't remember Leo ever being serious about anything, with the exception of physics and chemistry, at which he excelled. He couldn't play an instrument or sing a note, so he wasn't very welcome in the choir-camp counselor clique I hung out with. And, in spite of his large size, he wasn't very good at sports either. So, he did what he did best—he made everyone laugh.

We laughed a lot those few hours we had together in Nam. We rehashed the time Leo built a full-sized dummy caricature of Father John Crocker, our 1962 freshman Latin teacher. Using a pumpkin for a head, he stuffed a priest's cassock with newspapers and propped the dummy up in the front of the classroom. He draped it with a sign that read "The Bear," Father Crocker's nickname. Father Crocker hated the nickname, but seemed to enjoy the good-natured ribbing anyway. Of course, Leo had to be punished for his show of disrespect with a brief sentence on the detention brigade washing windows and cleaning blackboards. It was a small price to pay.

Over the two years since high school, we barely saw one another. We were both busy at college, he studying physics at John Carroll, a Jesuit university in Cleveland, and I at Kent. Joining the Marines seemed so out of character for him.

I pulled over to the curb in front of the familiar Heath home on Lake Street and sat there in my car admiring how the massive oaks in the front yard shrank the homestead to an intimate, human scale. Everything reflected order and care: the intricate workmanship in the 1920's brick facade, the polished brass gas light, the meticulously land-scaped yard and walkway, and the rich natural wood finish on the oversized front door.

I thought back on the last time I was at that house. It was in the summer of 1968 at a party Leo's parents threw for him when he was on two weeks' leave after completing his basic training at Parris Island. In the midst of his party, held in the basement, Leo pulled me aside and led me into the furnace room where we could talk in private. He spoke of his disenchantment with college and of questioning his faith, people in general, and politicians in particular.

"I got so confused about everything, Mike," he began. "And it wasn't the seminary that screwed me up, or college. It's that everything else seemed screwed up. Remember how in the 'sem' we learned to organize everything in terms of body, mind, and spirit?"

"Yeah, each principle was to be a platform for the others to thrive."

"That order fell apart for me. I lost my ability to sort out my life. With Vietnam coloring everything, college seemed like a joke. I'd attend a business class and think big business was about profiting either directly from the War or by diverting our attention from it by trying to sell us stuff we don't need. Meanwhile, guys our age are over there dying."

Again, we were on parallel tracks. "I know just what you mean, Leo."

"The Marines," he said, "restored my sense of purpose. Just like the seminary, the Corps taught attention to body, mind, and spirit too. For 'spirit,' they just mean patriotism, duty, and honor."

We shared our common doubts about the moral justification for the War, but he assured me of his new-found belief in the higher standards of the Marines. He had discovered a new home where he could strive to be his best. "I'm proud to be a Marine."

I took comfort in his certainty, since my military journey had also just begun. Unaware of his actions, I had enlisted about a month before his party and was due to go to Parris Island in a couple of months. This so delighted Leo he gave me another bear hug and wished me well with a "Semper Fi." When we returned to the main room, he was his party self again. He challenged everyone to a pushup contest and won easily.

During his surprise visit in Vietnam, we talked about his party as we sipped warm beers in the shade of my hooch. Leo had arrived in

Vietnam about six months before me and was promoted quickly to corporal as a machine gunner in a rifle company. When I brought up our conversation in his parents' basement furnace room, his face soured and he cast his eyes down. His reaction puzzled me. I asked him if he'd been in a lot a shit in Vietnam. All I got in response was an unfocused glare, like shell shock, the thousand yard stare.

As I walked up the manicured walkway toward the Heath's front door, I couldn't shake the memory of Leo's impenetrable stare. I had to replace those thoughts. I was about to spring a happy surprise on my old friend. First he'll shit a brick, I thought, and then we'll be pounding down cold brews for the rest of the day over stories.

I rang the front doorbell. When the church-like chimes finished announcing me, Mrs. Heath opened the heavy wooden door. She recognized me immediately but instead of greeting me, one hand moved up slowly to cover her mouth and the other found support on the frame of the screen door that separated us. She took a deep breath, arched her eyes and brows, and choked out an anguished sob. I waited silently, paralyzed by her keening, fearful of its meaning.

Recovered, but with the screen door still separating us, she began, "A few months after Leo got back, back from...Vietnam...he put a gun in his mouth...and fired. In his bedroom." The hand that covered her mouth swept across in front of her face. "Killed himself. Blood..." her words waned into fleeting images of Leo that swirled in my head; his laughs, his clowning style, his sincerity and sensitivity. He was the wise fool.

"I have to go now," she said abruptly. Whatever had held her up during the months since her son's suicide just could not do it anymore. Rather than collapse as the grief stabbed at her, she slowly closed the door in my face. She closed the heavy door on a chapter in my life, too. Still stunned, I mumbled that I was sorry, but she was no longer there to accept it. She had retreated behind the door. Its dark, carved wood sealed off all questions as effectively as Leo's thousand yard stare.

20

The Wall: Washington, D.C.; April 1971 and January 1991

Speak not to me of the glory of war, for I have stood in front of that black marble wall. I have held my father's hand as he searched for the names of friends he lost. I have felt the pain of remembrance. People talk now of honoring our troops—our veterans. If we are to truly do this, we have to remember them all, including those who have no memorial....

Honor our veterans by giving them a world where what they went through during war is not trivialized or made glamorous. Honor them by working to understand the consequences of war. Honor them by working to give them a world where they will never again have to stand at a wall and search for the names of their friends.

—Jessica A. Orange, from "Honor," 1991. Our daughter wrote these words after our visit to the Vietnam Veterans Memorial in January 1991.

April 23, 1971; Washington, D.C.

A huge procession of protesters, two hundred thousand strong, gathered at the steps to the Capital. A thousand of these protesters stood out from the others. They wore proof of service in Vietnam; long hair and green clothes; floppy green hats; jungle boots; uniforms of green, blue, red, and black. They wore ribbons and medals on their chests and around their necks, symbols made of precious metals and colorful satin, symbols awarded for having served their country in wartime, for sacrificing their time and their labor. Many sacrificed more—their patriotism, their sense of honor and duty, their self-respect, their sanity. Some left friends, senses, and limbs in Vietnam, others lost their souls there. They had only these symbols and a sense of betrayal to show for it. It would be eleven years before their country would build its first national monument to those who made the ultimate sacrifice in service to their country during the War.

One by one they stepped forward to a microphone placed before a fence erected at the base of the Capital steps. One by one, they spoke a few heartfelt words into the microphone and, in an act enriched with more symbolism than the medals and ribbons they held in their hands, they cast these symbols back at the headquarters of the government that awarded them. For the first time in this country's history, men who fought a war protested to end it.

As jumbled as my convictions were at the time of my enlistment, my war experience jumbled them even more. Post-Vietnam life in the land of plenty didn't help either. Every day I tried to turn off the Vietnam movie that ran through my head. Change channels; channel change. I was a closet veteran. I came to that Washington demonstration as a passive observer, with friends who accepted me in spite of the fact I couldn't accept myself. I left as a member of the group that organized the protest, the Vietnam Veterans Against the War.

January 1991; Washington, D.C.

After two decades of political involvement, Cynthia and I returned to Washington, D.C., this time with our daughter, Jessica. We were there to march for peace in the Middle East. Jessica had been with us on protests for liberal causes since she was a baby and several on her own, but this was her first in the nation's capital. She was eighteen.

We made a pilgrimage to the Vietnam Veterans Memorial. After a time, Cynthia suggested that Jessica and I stand at either end of the panels that listed the dead during my tour of duty—March 1969 to March 1970. Cynthia snapped a picture of these 365 days of death. The black polished granite panels numbers thirteen to thirty-one towered well beyond the reach of my hand. That year engulfed a major portion of the monument's inscriptions. I wondered how many sons died because they wanted to prove themselves worthy of their fathers.

I wanted to find John Kitson's name, my friend from boot camp and Advanced Infantry Training school. The monument's directory gave the following information: John Frances Kitson, Pfc., 18 July 50, 23 July 69, Levittown, NY. He died five days after his nineteenth birthday, a little over four months after we both had arrived in Vietnam. The monument didn't mention his glory days on the 1964 varsity lacrosse team at Gen. Douglas MacArthur High school in Levittown or the family that survived him.

I decided to do a pencil rubbing of his name from that ominously powerful wall. "J...O...H..." I only got that far. Seeing the individual letters emerge from the white sheet to create that name—to conjure up that skinny teenager—ignited such sorrow in me. I struggled to complete the task through eyes burning with tears. I liked Kitson in boot camp where I got to know him. He had a New York tough-guy attitude that was probably just a thin cover for the deep fear we all harbored while training for warfare. I hadn't just lost a friend. I lost a piece of myself in that damnable War. I was crying for myself.

I turned to Cynthia and Jessica for the embrace and acceptance I desperately needed. I cried uncontrollably on my daughter's shoulder.

In their arms, I experienced an out-of-body sensation that placed the three of us in the middle of the scene. In this mental picture, I saw two women consoling a gray-bearded man holding a crumpled rubbing and dressed in faded jeans, a "Veterans for Peace" cap, and a Marine Corps field jacket bedecked with peace buttons and twenty-year-old stains. I realized we were inadvertently reenacting the typical Wall scene so often pictured in the media.

I returned to the massive gravestone and searched for Leo's name. When I could not find the engraving that would help to commemorate his life and his service, I asked for the help of a Park Ranger.

"There are no suicides on the Wall, only deaths directly related to the War."

Had I known then that more men killed themselves after the War than are listed on it, I would have told the Ranger we'd need another memorial for the sixty thousand suicides that would not have happened were it not for the War. For the sixty thousand Leos.

21

Caution in the Waking

Waking Him

Careful not to startle him,
She tip-toes into the room and watches. His eyes
Are squeezed shut and twitch slightly
With the intensity of his sleep.

Quietly, she calls him
"Daddy...Daddy are you sleeping?"
She has learned to wake him slowly.
If she is too sudden, he will uncoil
A fierce spring rusted loose.

Gently, she must nudge him back
Into the world of fenced-in yards
And refrigerator art, away
From the shadowy echoes of rotten canvas and death.

She knows her child hand is not enough,
Because even she is in some of those dreams.
Staggering with him shoeless through mud.
That is all he will say. He tries

To protect her, but she hears
The screams at night. She already knows.

She must use caution in the waking.

Dreams

She watches me sleep.
I know this, and I know
She approaches me with the heart
Of a bird that flutters
More than it beats.
And I know this is because
She is afraid (must be afraid)
Of my sleep.

I know this because she is there
with me sometimes,
staggering through the mud and confusion.
There is no safe place,
No way to escape the smell and the death,
Or the quiet in my right ear.

With her I am NEVER angry, because
With the heart of a bird
She is afraid of my sleep.

—Jessica A. Orange, 1990

Over there, I made myself stop thinking of everything back here. When I got back here, it didn't work the other way around. A whiff of diesel exhaust, the two-dimensional light of a full moon, the buzz of flies, a marijuana buzz, sound of a helicopter, wet feet, crowds, loud noises—all sparked flashbacks. I was even dangerous to wake up. A few days after returning home, my little brother, Joe, tried to wake me one morning by shaking my shoulder instead of hitting the bottoms of my feet, as was the custom in Vietnam. I awoke on the floor on top of him with both my hands strangling his ten-year-old neck, his eyes bugged out in terror. For nearly two decades after returning home, thoughts of Vietnam began my every day. Dreams, many of them violent, plagued my nights and frightened my wife and daughter. What follows is one of them:

In the dream, I was in a military or police uniform and on a mission with two others. He was somewhat short, thin, and wiry, with sandy-blonde hair. She was shorter still and stocky. Both were in their mid-forties. I had a pistol, if you could call it that. It looked so tiny in its black holster. Instead of a strong wide belt, a thin black strap with a buckle kept it from sliding off my hips. I slid it around in front of my crotch like a codpiece. It provided little self assurance.

We were to go into a building to secure it, round up all the people, and detain them. I knew nothing more. Next, I was alone in a long corridor lined on both sides with small doorways. I walked slowly down the dimly lit hallway and peered into each of the rooms. They were small, most lit by a single yellowing lamp. All were empty save for a few that had old upright pianos. At the end of the hall was a staircase.

When I had returned to the front end of the hallway, I heard someone leave a room. I turned and saw the back of a man. He was short, heavy, and had closely cropped hair and a massive neck. His wide head blended into his neck and then into his broad shoulders. His dark skin made me wonder if he was a fair-skinned African American or an Asian man.

In a loud, firm voice, I ordered "Halt!" He slowly turned. The most prominent feature was a huge wide grin framing large bright teeth with spaces in between. His round face and dark complexion exaggerated the whiteness and size of his eyes and their black pupils.

His grin turned to a scowl. He emanated spite and insolence as he ignored my order, turned, and walked in a sashay-like waddle toward the rear stairway. I moved to follow and caught up to him as he was halfway down the stairs. I ordered him to halt and again he turned and glared at me with those huge eyes and grimace.

Next I was running after him in the open and I began to gain on him. I leapt after him and floated magically through the air. The sensation was wonderful and free. I flew right up to him at shoulder level, threw my right arm around in front, with my wrist and thumb tensed like steel, and struck with all my might into his larynx. Instinctively, my left arm came up on the left side of his neck and grasped my right hand in handshake fashion. I pulled with all my might to cut off the blood flow through both of his carotid arteries and bent my head down on the back of his to force his head down.

This was the naked-death-strangle-hold I learned in boot camp. The intent was to kill silently within two or three minutes. The problem was, the maneuver required the weight of the attacker to collapse the victim in a doubled over posture that exacerbated the tension on the neck and effectively cut off air and blood to the brain. I was still floating in a position horizontal to my victim, weightless. Despite my iron-hard grip, the head slowly turned and those piercing white saucer eyes bore into me. The sardonic grin, unchanged, mocked me.

Somehow, he propelled me away and I fell in a heap on the ground a few feet in front of him. He drew slowly closer and I pulled out my tiny pistol and aimed it at his head. He continued toward me, his pasted-on facial expression never changing. I pulled the trigger just as I had so often in Vietnam, slowly without knowing when the steel of the trigger will clear the hammer and let it snap down on the firing pin. My mind's eye filled with the action of that trigger. It moved in slow motion all the way to the rear of the trigger housing and stopped when it hit metal.

The image returned to the confrontation and I saw a minute bullet leave the end of the stubby barrel. The bullet became an ever lengthening rod that moved from the gun toward the man. At the instant the rod touched the upper right side of the man's forehead, the action shifted to real time. I heard the blast of the gun, felt the kick, and my view became clouded by the flame and smoke from the barrel.

The smoke cleared just as I saw the upper right side of the man's head vaporize. A moment later, a bloody mass of purplish flesh was exposed. His demeanor never changed, it was as though nothing had happened.

Then I noticed his hands reaching for the little pistol with fingers fibrillating like a centipede's legs. They gently redirected the barrel toward the man's mid-chest. The grimace softened somewhat and I fired a second time and woke up.

I have had many violent dreams, most of which left me drenched in sweat and emotion. This one was unique in that I was completely detached throughout and even after awakening.

My violent dreams stopped after the first draft of this book. Writing exorcised my demons and opened me to the love and acceptance from family and friends.

22

For the Next Generation

Throughout our history, our profoundest ideology, the pervasive feeling among our people, has been patriotism. Whatever the odds, we would have continued to fight. Another twenty years, even one hundred years, as long as it took it to win—regardless of cost."

—General Vo Nguyen Giap,
Commander in Chief for the North Vietnamese Army

The problem with telling a war story is the issue of scale. Hollywood and the evening news desensitize us all. There is a fundamental difference between observing the chaos and mayhem of war from an easy chair instead of a foxhole or gunship. With every telling, Hollywood has escalated the typical war story to include huge firefights, atrocities, betrayal, carpet bombing, the death of buddies, and an atomized body every minute. The media typically delivers few human-scaled war stories, only big bloody ones.

I've read a lot about the Vietnam War so I know many men experienced and perpetrated horrors far beyond anything I saw. Most vets, even combat vets, had far less grand experiences, myself included. I felt a strange dichotomy for many years. I experienced things that scarred my soul, but I was embarrassed to talk about them because they didn't seem as traumatic as what I knew others went through. I felt my experiences didn't warrant telling. I was caught in a dilemma. How could I be a brave, strong Marine, yet also be the victim of emotional pain and suffering? I also feared that admitting the War had damaged me would lead people to assume I had seen and done despicable things that fit the "baby killer" stereotype for the Vietnam vet. It was easier to never admit I served. Denial was a safer way to avoid the undertow of the War.

In 1984, fourteen years after I returned home from Vietnam, I began addressing elementary and high school students about my experiences and my thoughts on the politics of the War. The invitation to speak became an annual late spring ritual when the high school American history teachers, having spent the year on the Revolutionary War, Civil War, and this century's two World Wars, crammed my war in those fitful few days before finals and the coveted summer break. My task was to demystify the cartoon-like Rambo movies that all the kids had seen and enliven the confusing mush of socio-historical snippets found in the two pages their history book devoted to my generation's precious coming-of-age era. I had fifty minutes.

Typically, one of the first questions I get is, "Did you kill anybody?" I remember the first time was during the first class I addressed. It was in 1984 before my daughter's seventh grade Social Studies class and it came from a little girl who delivered the question like a blow to my sternum. I stammered through quivering lips and chin, "Yes, I killed people. That was my job. To kill people." That was the first time I verbalized the truth. It was the last time my answer sent tears down my cheeks and caused my psyche to hyperventilate. Confession has its merits.

What follows is a selection of the concepts I typically relate in the classroom:

The "Morally Ambiguous War"

My generation's war, Vietnam, was America's longest war. It is often compared to the war of my parents' generation, World War II, America's "Good War." To the historians, the Vietnam War was different because it was a "morally ambiguous war." To the combatants of any war, the three-word phrase, "morally ambiguous war," is redundant. The notion is naive because war, by its very nature, requires individuals to do things that are morally ambiguous.

War takes the adage "the end does not justify the means" and turns it on its head. Fundamental to war is the justification of any means for a desired end. All wars cause horrible consequences for both combatants and civilians, for both the perpetrators of the violence and their victims. The modern rules of war like the Geneva Convention are attentive to the means of waging war. They represent crucial civilizing advancements, but they have their limits. For example, the Geneva Convention condemns mass executions but accepts carpet bombing although the results—the ends—are similar for both means of warmaking. I believe that for the bombardier over Dresden as well as for the infantry grunt at My Lai, the rules of war can feel like artificial boundaries around what is essentially socially sanctioned barbarism.

The anguish that results from that moral ambiguity has a self-correcting effect that can help to limit warfare. A much worse thing is killing with moral certainty. Consider the Islamic Jihads, the Christian Crusades and Inquisition, the recent religious wars in the Middle East, Northern Ireland, Africa, and the Balkans—the list can go on and on. Only moral certainty is capable of creating the needed laser-like fortitude of body, mind, and spirit for an individual to help make a death camp work.

In his remarkable book, *On Killing: The Psychological Cost of Learning to Kill in War and Society*, Lt. Col. David Grossman describes how differently we feel about atrocity and war. He writes, "We cannot understand how anyone could perform...inhuman atrocities on their fellow man.

We call it murder, and we hunt down and prosecute the criminals responsible, be they Nazi war criminals or American war criminals. And by prosecuting these individuals, we gain peace of mind by affirming to ourselves that this is an aberration that civilized societies do not tolerate. But when most people think of those who bombed Hamburg or Hiroshima, there is no feeling of disgust for the deed, certainly not the intensity of disgust felt for Nazi executioners....We rationalize their actions and most of us have a gut feeling that we could have done what the bomber crews did, but could not ever had done what the executioners did." Again, there is little distinction in the results on the ground.

As a society, we want both our means and our ends to be just, but war will never pass the smell test. The essence of life is that it thrives only by killing and eating. War is a natural outgrowth of this essence. The dualism that is at the heart of Western philosophy creates an expectation that there can be something essentially "good" and something else essentially "bad." Eastern philosophy instead talks about the inter-connectedness and interdependence of all things and letting go of all illusions. As the Yin-Yang symbol so aptly illustrates, the dark part of the circle intertwines with the light part, and at the heart of each part is a smaller circle of the opposite shade. This is inter-connection or "inter-being," as the Vietnamese Buddhist monk and author, Thich Nhat Hanh, calls it.

Ralph Peters, an author and strategist who retired as an Army colonel last year, spoke on this issue. "This is not a matter of condoning 'war crimes.' It's a matter of understanding the...speed, confusion, terror and eruptive violence of warfare. An army should be as moral as practical, but to me, war is by its very nature a fundamentally immoral act. So this is a matter of degrees, not absolutes."

In the midst of these dilemmas, society requires our young adults to don uniforms and to implement, without question, the means of war with little regard for the ends. Thirty-two years ago, I was one of those young adults. As a soldier in Vietnam, I did my job like any other combat soldier in any other war. My job was to kill people.

In his book, *On Killing*, David Grossman provides compelling evidence about the nature of humanity. He describes military studies that demonstrated how we humans have a powerful, innate resistance toward killing other humans. I found the message very heartening. Then he proceeds to explain the great strides the military has made to develop the psychological mechanisms to overcome that innate resistance. The studies examined the firing rates of soldiers in battle and found that for World War II, only fifteen to twenty percent of the combat troops fired their weapons at the enemy. I was amazed by the results of the study. Four out of five soldiers did not fire their weapons at the enemy in battle. This led to better training for the Korean War soldier and a resultant increase to a fifty-five percent firing rate. In Vietnam, the American soldier was psychologically enabled to kill to a far greater degree than any soldier in history, a remarkable firing rate of ninety to ninety-five percent. This military accomplishment created a psychic deficit in the soldiers; the more developed each soldier's conscience, the greater the deficit. Instead, Vietnam veterans, in Grossman's words, "were denied the…essential purification ritual that is a part of every warrior society, and finally [were] condemned and accused by [their] own society to a degree that is unprecedented in Western history." The effects of Vietnam were like nuclear fallout: You can't see, hear, smell, taste, or feel it, but it can poison you to death.

The historian, Myra MacPherson, wrote about Vietnam, the first war America ever lost, and said, "America lost its virginity in Vietnam." For three decades we have grappled with the significance of this loss like Germany has had to deal with its role and defeat in the two world wars of the last century. To the victors go the spoils and, more importantly, the right to define the "morality" of the effort.

The Hero's Journey

After nearly three decades of silence about my experiences in Vietnam, I found the Hero's Journey model and it has helped me to understand and integrate my experiences. The model involves five stages beginning with (1) a hero who, out of a sense of duty and honor, (2) undertakes a mission or quest. The hero endures a difficult test during the journey and accomplishes a valued mission, or at least makes a heroic effort, or dies trying. The hero (3) grows from the experience and (4) returns home with something the community values, and this is, at least ideally, then answered by the community in (5) welcoming the hero back home. The model works for many of the myths that are foundational to our cultural heritage, including the adolescent rite of passage.

The first stage involves the hero, someone who commits to something bigger than himself or herself. The hero is willing to transcend thinking of self-preservation and undergo what author, Joseph Campbell, calls "a transformation of consciousness,...a redemption."

Stage two, the quest, is a series of adventures and tests that are beyond the ordinary. It's a cycle, a going and a returning, the death of one life (for example childhood and adolescence) and the birth of the next (adulthood). Childbirth, for example, fits this pattern perfectly, with the mother giving over of her life for the life of another, the rigors of pregnancy, and the pain of the birth process. It is definitely a heroic deed. For men, going off to war is just as timeless an example.

Cultures throughout history require that young men experience the warrior's quest as a rite of passage, an initiation rite to manhood. The hero leaves the realm of the familiar and descends into a dark unknown. There the hero learns important things, basic things about life, and the incredible range of human behavior. The warrior puts on a uniform and becomes a different creature. This is stage three. When I was a young man, I wanted a test, a dangerous mission that would help me prove to my father, my girlfriend, and especially to myself that I was tough and brave, or at least not a coward.

My experiences in Vietnam took me to the frontiers of my humanity where I wet my pants in terror, I wallowed in self pity, I fueled my hatred, I raged in anger, I reveled in the arrogance of my firepower, and I drank in the sweet elation of survival as deeply as I did the raw thrill of killing. No other experience was as crammed full of meaning. I still struggle to fathom its full significance. The experience is

unknowable remotely. Movies, television, and literature offer only vir-
tual war, a vicarious taste of the terror, the blood lust, and the thrill of
participation, but without the risk, and without the risk, it just isn't the
experience of war.

Stage four brings in the larger community. It's at this point that the
Hero's Journey model broke down for the Vietnam veteran. Society
has the responsibility to judge the value of the quest. The poet,
Archibald MacLeish, speaks to this in his famous poem, "The Young
Dead Soldiers." He has the young dead soldiers say to society "We
leave you our deaths. Give them their meaning." Well, America gave
us the meaning of Vietnam. She decided it was at best a horrible and
unfortunate mistake, and probably immoral. That condemnation poisoned the quest and the warriors. For decades I was plagued by the
question, could soldiering be moral in an immoral war? Now I realize
the moral ambiguity that is inherent to all wars makes that question
irrelevant to the combatant.

As a young man, I bought the argument that we were there to
defend the Vietnamese from a Communist takeover, but what I saw
there was a people seeking their liberation from all outside forces. In
her book, *When Heaven and Earth Changed Places*, Le Ly Heyslip
describes her experiences as a Vietnamese peasant and how she suffered at the hands of all three sides in the War—the Communists, the
U.S. forces, and the army we came to help, the South Vietnamese
army:

> If you were an American GI, I ask you to…look into the heart
> of one you once called enemy.…For you, [the War] was a sim-
> ple thing: Democracy against Communism. For us, that was
> not our fight at all. How could it be? We knew little of
> Democracy and even less about Communism. For most of us, it
> was a fight for independence—like the American Revolution.
>
> The least you did—the least any of us did—was our duty. For
> that we must be proud.…In the war many Americans—and

many more Vietnamese—lost limbs, loved ones, and that little light we see in babies' eyes which is our own hope for the future. Do not despair. As long as you are alive, that light still burns within you.

I could not look at a Vietnamese man, woman—or two boys rummaging through our garbage—and know whether they were the people I was sent to liberate from Communism, or kill. It is fundamental to "know your enemy." We did not. Tactics deteriorated to free-fire zones and the policy of shooting anything that moved. With numbed consciences, morale and morals followed the same decayed path until we viewed the Vietnamese as less than human. We rationalized "destroying villages in order to save them."

I couldn't help but be jealous of the welcome the country awarded people like my parents when they and so many others returned home from military service after World War II. They returned with the prize of having preserved democracy and freed the world from the threat of tyranny. Their newly acquired knowledge of the stuff of life was of great value to the rest of the community and the country honored them appropriately. However, for the returning Vietnam combat veteran, both society and the veterans saw nothing of value to share. There was only pain, frustration, and anguish. Instead of being treated as heroes, they were shunned by the World War II and Korean War vets for losing the war, by the Hippies for being war mongers, and by themselves for being duped by their country.

I often get the question "If you could go back in time, what would you do now?" I answer that if I had then the wisdom and experience I have now, I would choose to be a different hero on a different quest. I would avoid the quagmire that was Vietnam and instead seek my rite of passage to manhood through peaceful means. I would want my Hero's Journey to be more harmonious with my values, for example, through a stint with the Peace Corps. I don't think I'd avoid the draft by using my middle-class privileges, but maybe I would resist it actively and conscientiously, and even go to jail if necessary. Maybe I would dedicate myself to stopping the War and the senseless killing. I respect those who did.

The Vietnamese were too determined to ever be defeated by a foreign force, no matter how powerful. Defense of their homeland was a sacred obligation. The good that came of the antiwar effort at home exceeded the pain it caused. It weakened the American fighting spirit and emboldened our enemy's. As a result, our inevitable defeat came quicker and with less loss of life for all sides of the conflict.

In order to sensitize the kids I speak to about the problems many returning Vietnam combat vets faced, I give them a hypothetical question. "If you wanted to make a vet crazy and had no limits to your power and authority, how would you do it?" I answer my own question with the following list based upon the testimony of Dr. John P. Wilson before the U.S. Senate Committee on Veteran Affairs in 1980:

• I would grab a boy right after high school and send him to an unpopular war far away from home.

• I'd be sure to exempt any friends he had that were headed to college so they could mount a demoralizing antiwar movement back home.

• I'd create a one-year tour of duty and have each soldier come and go on an individual schedule in order to prevent the formation of a cohesive unit with high morale. This would also work against the desirable sense of purpose to win the war as a noble cause worth fighting for and instead foster a survivor mentality.

• I'd expose him to intensely stressful events, some so horrible that it would be impossible for him to talk about them later to anyone except his fellow survivors.

• But then, when his tour of duty was up, I'd fly him home without an opportunity to sort out the meaning of his experiences with his fellow survivors.

• Instead of the expected homecoming welcome or victory parades, I'd make sure that the public media stigmatized him and portrayed him as a "drug-crazed psychopathic killer."

•   Then I'd make sure the Veterans Administration system of hospitals would lack adequate services for him.

•   Since I grabbed him right after high school, he won't be able to easily reenter the mainstream of society because he's undereducated and lacks marketable job skills. So I'd cut back on the GI Bill program and make it more difficult for him to get that needed education.

•   Finally, I'd drop him into an economy suffering from high inflation and unemployment.

•   If all of this didn't do the job, I'd get society to convince him to feel isolated, stigmatized, unappreciated, and exploited for volunteering to serve his country.

I close this point by telling the students that this scenario was not fictitious; it was the homecoming for most Vietnam veterans.

Many Vietnam veterans did poorly for many years after the war. Stage five of the "Hero's Journey," the hero's welcome home, was a bust. We suffered all of the pain but savored none of the glory. We received condemnations instead of congratulations. I had a growing suspicion it was all for nothing. Many, like me, were caught in a limbo between a war that was over and a society that was disturbed by our story. I felt like an exile in my own country. Using 1993 statistics that compared Vietnam vets to their peers, author, Dr. Daryl Paulson, reports that alcohol and drug abuse were five times greater among the vets, the divorce rate was four times greater, unemployment was three times greater, and suicides nearly three times greater.

I fully recognize that the primary stressor on the combatants of all wars is the moral ambiguity of having to kill for any cause. The resulting psychological wounds can completely overwhelm the healing ability of the larger society to help the returning veteran reintegrate into society. You just can't compare the healing power of a parade to the poisonous power of having caused death. We Vietnam vets may even have an advantage over our predecessors from other wars. Society is more open now to talking about these things and we have the benefit of healing professionals who are smarter about things like post traumatic stress disorder.

Experts describe how severe trauma can explode the cohesion of consciousness and that detailed journaling that exposes the full spectrum of emotions that the events arouse can help the survivor to rebuild the ruins of character. This book changed me. The writing taught me how much I did learn and grow from my choices and my military experience. I have come to accept and reintegrate a part of me that I had tried divorcing from my personality for nearly thirty years. As a direct result of Vietnam and its effects on the three decades that followed it, I do have something to offer my community. This book is testament. As I've come to more publicly accept my role, my family, friends and larger community have responded with a more intimate version of the hero's welcome.

Recently, an older boy in a class asked if I knew anybody who had a hard time when they got back. I answered yes and urged the class to talk to veterans. "We want to tell our stories but we have to feel safe. Start with easy questions such as what did you wear, what did you eat, what did you do on holidays? Start out slowly but don't give up too easily. Ask with a loving heart." I started to tell the class Leo's story, highlighting the contrast of our seminary days to our war experiences. I got to the part of the story where I knocked on Leo's parents' front door, mimicked the knock for the kids, and broke into tears. Embarrassed, I turned my back to them and tried to rein in my hyperventilating emotions. I completely surprised myself. I thought I had a handle on this stuff. Turning back to face my impressionable audience, I intended to repeat Mrs. Heath's words to me but I could only squeak the words out between my own choked sobs and sniffles. Then I noticed two boys in the back left corner of the classroom snickering to one another. Their frivolity helped me regain control. I finished the story slowly and carefully.

The class ended a few minutes later and the room emptied for the lunch bell in about four seconds, except for one older girl who stood staring at the floor a few feet in front of me. I asked her if she had a question. She said nothing but took a step closer. I asked if she was all right and she replied in a soft voice, holding back emotion.

"My dad was in Vietnam."

"Oh, is he OK?"

After a long pause, she said, "He killed himself...I was six."

Her tears re-triggered mine and we hugged.

"I'm sorry. I'm sorry," I told her. "The War screwed up people over there and long after they got back. It is still hurting people. Some things can't be wept away."

*   *   *

Society's role concerning the Vietnam War is to try to understand the warriors who have been poisoned once by combat, and once again by society's condemnation of them and their war. During our morally ambiguous tours of duty, we Vietnam veterans were in the hands of war, a long long way from home. Since then, we've been in society's hands. Too many of us are still trying to find our way home. Help us come the rest of the way.

Remember us.

THE END

Chronology of Milestones in the Book (in bold face) and Major World Events (in *italics*)

1950..................Ho Chi Minh declares Vietnam independence. China and the
                      U.S.S.R. recognize Ho Chi Minh as Vietnam's leader. The
                      U.S. and Britain recognize Bao Dai as Vietnam's leader.
                      President Truman commits $15 million to French war effort
                      in Indochina.

1950..................Start of the Korean War.

5/54 ....Dienbienphu falls to the Vietminh. Geneva Conference calls
                      for temporary division of Vietnam into north and south sec-
                      tors to relieve hostilities, and elections in two years to reunify
                      country. U.S. commits $100 million in aid to government of
                      South Vietnam. Refugees flee from North to South Vietnam
                      aided by the U.S. navy. Bao Dai selects Ngo Dinh Diem as
                      Prime Minister of South Vietnam.

1955..................U.S. agrees to finance and train South Vietnamese army.
                      Diem, backed by U.S., refuses to participate in elections
                      called for in Geneva Agreements.

1958..................The USSR orbits Sputnik, the first satellite.

7/59 ....Two American servicemen killed in Vietnam by guerrillas.

1960..................South Vietnamese leaders voice opposition to Diem's repres-
                      sive government.

1961...................*President Kennedy sends first Green Beret advisors to Vietnam.*

9/61-6/66..........I attended St. Charles Borromeo Seminary in Cleveland, Ohio.

1961...................*The USSR puts the first man in space.*

1961...................*The Freedom Ride buses are burned in Alabama.*

1962...................*American Military Assistance Command established in Vietnam. Twelve thousand advisors in country.*

10/62 ....*The Cuban Missile Crisis.*

1963...................*Assassination of civil right leader, Medgar Evers.*

5-8/63 ....*Vietnamese Buddhist monks stage peace demonstrations and self-immolations.*

9/63 ....*Fall and assassination of President Ngo Dinh Diem in Saigon.*

11/63.................*President John F. Kennedy is assassinated in Dallas.*

8/64 ....*Incident involving U.S. destroyer, Maddox, in Tonkin Gulf prompts passage of Tonkin Gulf Resolution by Congress. U.S. bombs North Vietnam for the first time.*

10/64 ....*China explodes atomic bomb.*

1964...................*Congress passes the Civil Rights Act.*

12/31/64 ...........*U.S. military personnel in Vietnam: 23,300*
Killed in action to date:.....................................267
Wounded in action to date:...........................1,534

2/65 ....*President Johnson orders Operation Rolling Thunder, a massive bombing campaign of North Vietnam.*

3/65 ....*First regular U.S. combat troops in Vietnam (two Marine battalions).*

4/65 ....*Students for a Democratic Society stage major antiwar protest in Washington, D.C.*

5/65 ....I take the side favoring U.S. military involvement in Vietnam War in high school debate.

1965...................*Malcolm X assassinated.*

1966...................*M.L. King speaks out against the Vietnam War.*

6/66 ....Just before high school graduation, I decided against going on to the seminary college to become a Catholic priest and instead enrolled in the architecture program at Kent State University (KSU) in Kent, Ohio.

9/66 ....I began the architecture preparatory program at KSU. Because of dormitory housing shortages, I lived in my family's eight-by-thirty-five-foot travel trailer in a trailer park about three miles from the campus. I began dating for the first time.

12/31/66 ...........*U.S. military personnel in Vietnam: 385,380*
Killed in action to date:....................................... 6,644
Wounded in action to date:.............................. 37,738

8/67 ....**Race riots in numerous American cities. I was nearly caught in Cleveland's.**

1967..................*Che Guevara assassinated.*

1967..................*North Vietnam vows to negotiate for peace once U.S. stops bombing.*

8/67 ....**I met Bridget at a wedding. We began dating.**

10/67 ....*March on the Pentagon by fifty thousand antiwar protesters.*

12/67 ....**"The Inquisition" at my family's home over my sleeping with Bridget.**

1/68 ....*North Vietnamese and Viet Cong troops launch Tet (New Year) Offensive. Battle of Khe Sanh.*

2/68 ....*The battle for Hue. General Westmoreland requests 206,000 additional troops.*

3/68 ....*President Johnson announces intention not to run for re-election after nearly losing the New Hampshire primary to antiwar candidate Sen. Eugene McCarthy.*

4/68 .................*M.L. King assassinated in Memphis.*

5/68 ....*Start of the Paris Peace Talks.*

6/68 ....*Robert Kennedy assassinated in Los Angeles.*

1968..................*Antiwar demonstrations and police riots mark the Democratic National Convention in Chicago.*

7/68 ....After completing my second year at Kent State and being placed on academic on probation, I became disillusioned with life in general, and joined the Marines. I also attended a party for my friend, Leo Heath, at his parents' house just before his departure for Vietnam

8/68 ....I took a trip with three friends from the seminary to New York City. There I met Cynthia from St. Paul, Minnesota. We met on the Observation Deck of the Empire State Building and spent the entire night together riding the subways, visiting Coney Island, and talking like two old friends.

9/68-3/69..........I completed basic training at the Marines Corps Recruit Depot in Parris Island, South Carolina (mid September to late December); Camp Geiger in Charlotte, North Carolina (after Christmas to early February); and Camp Pendleton near Oceanside, California (mid-February to early March).

11/68.................*Richard Nixon defeats Hubert Humphrey for the Presidency.*

12/68 ....*First draft lottery since 1942.*

12/31/68 ...........*U.S. military personnel in Vietnam: 536,100*
Killed in action to date:...30,610
Wounded in action to date:....................................192,850

1/69 ....North Koreans seize the U.S.S. Pueblo. I was in training and fearful I would be sent to Korea in the winter instead of to Vietnam.

3/69 ....*President Nixon begins secret bombing of alleged North Vietnamese Army camps in Cambodia.*

3/17/69 ....I arrived in Vietnam and was assigned to an 81 mm mortar platoon with the First Marine Division's First Regiment, First Battalion in the vicinity of Da Nang.

3/69 ....*A federal grand jury indicts the "Chicago Eight" for conspiracy to incite a riot during the 1968 Democratic National Convention in Chicago.*

3/69 ....*A Gallup pole records thirty-two percent of Americans favor greatly escalating the War or "going all out," twenty-six percent favor pulling out, nineteen percent favor continuation of the current policy, and twenty-one percent have no opinion.*

4/69 ....Leo Heath visited me at my base.

5/69 ....I was promoted to Lance Corporal and assigned as squad leader for the First Squad in the Second Section after Cowboy rotated home.

5/69 ....I participated in Operation Pipestone Canyon.

6/69 ....*First man on the moon, Neil Armstrong.*

8/69 ....I received Meritorious Combat Promotion to Corporal for performance during Operation Durham Peak in the Que Son Mountains.

1969..................*Woodstock.*

9/69 ....*President Ho Chi Minh dies.*

9/69 ....*Criminal charges formally preferred against Lt. William Calley for the massacre of 109 "Oriental human beings" at My Lai in March 1968.*

10/69 ....*A Gallup pole reports that sixty-seven percent of Americans favor the withdrawal of all Americans from Vietnam by the end of 1970.*

10/69 ....*President Nixon announces draft deferment for graduate students.*

11/69..................*Two hundred fifty thousand protesters in Washington, D.C. stage the largest antiwar protest in the nation's history. President Nixon begins "phased withdrawal" of troops from Vietnam.*

1/70 ....I was assigned as Section Leader for the Second Section.

3/70 ....I spent the last three weeks of my tour of duty training new mortarmen and living in a bunker under my hooch.

3/70 ....I left Vietnam and spent two days in Okinawa in transit to Camp Pendleton.

3/70 ....I returned to my family's home in Cleveland, Ohio and discovered the next day that my girl friend, Bridget, was pregnant (obviously not from me).

3/70 ....My father secured a deckhand job for me on the Great Lakes Fleet ore carrier, the *D. M. Clemson.*

1970.................*Senate holds hearings on the Equal Rights Amendment.*

5/3/70 ....*President Nixon announces "Cambodian Incursion."*

5/2 ....I visited Bridget in the hospital the day of her twenty-second birthday and the day she gave birth to the girl she would give up to Catholic Charities for adoption.

5/2 ....I returned to Kent State University to find the campus in turmoil over President Nixon's invasion of Cambodia.

5/4 ....While I was trying to catch my ship in Detroit, the Ohio National Guardsmen on May 4 shot thirteen students, killing four.

6/70 ....I jumped ship in Duluth and hitchhiked to St. Paul to visit Cynthia for two days.

9/70 ....I visited the Heath home to see my friend Leo. Leo's mother told me he had committed suicide months after returning from Vietnam.

10/70 ....I married Bridget.

12/31/70 ...........*U.S. military personnel in Vietnam: 334,600*
Killed in action to date: 44,245
Wounded in action to date:...................................293,439

3/71 ....*Lt. Calley convicted of premeditated murder of Vietnamese civilians in 1968.*

4/71..................I traveled with friends to Washington, D.C. for a major protest and observed the Vietnam Vets Against the War throw their medals away in protest of the War. I begin my involvement in the antiwar movement.

6/71 ....The New York Times *publishes* The Pentagon Papers, *a secret history of U.S. involvement in Vietnam, made public by Daniel Ellsberg.*

6/71 ....Bridget and I separated.

6/71-6/73 ....I lived a life that included a dozen jobs.

3/72 ....*Jessica is born to Cynthia.*

6/72 ....*Watergate break-in.*

1972..................*President Nixon orders intensive bombing of North Vietnam as peace talks fail.*

7/72 ....Cynthia left her husband and moved to St. Paul.

11/72..................Bridget and I tried to make the marriage work but one month later we filed do-it-yourself, no-fault divorce papers, I renewed my Merchant Marines papers, and departed Kent for New Orleans to find a ship and sail around the world.

11/72..................*President Nixon defeats George McGovern for the Presidency.*

1/73 ....*Cease fire agreements signed in Paris. End of military draft.*

3/73 ..................*U.S. completes withdrawal of combat troops from Vietnam. American prisoners of war released.*

1973..................*War Powers Act passed over President Nixon's veto.*

1973..................*Allende is overthrown and assassinated in Chile.*

6/73 ....Came to St. Paul to work a railroad construction job and live with Cynthia and Jessica so we could make a final decision regarding our relationship.

7/21/73 ....The three of us were married.

9/73-6/74 ....We moved to Kent and I finished my last year and a half of school.

5/74 ....*Fighting resumes in South Vietnam. Impeachment hearings for President Nixon.*

6/74 ....We returned to Minnesota and I returned to my railroad construction job.

8/74 ....*Nixon resigns as President.*

3/75 ....I got my first professional job as an airport planner trainee in St. Paul.

4/75 ....Last Americans (press and diplomatic personnel) are evacu-
ated from South Vietnam. The North Vietnamese Army cap-
tures Saigon and the Vietnam War ends.

**3/76 ....I became a city planner with the Minneapolis
Planning Department.**

1976..................North and South Vietnam are united into one country, the
Socialist republic of Vietnam.

1/77 ....One day after his inauguration, President Carter grants
amnesty to most of the 10,000 Vietnam War draft resisters.
Total U.S. war casualties:
Killed and missing in action: 58,132
 Wounded in action: 303,704

11/82..................The Vietnam Veterans memorial is dedicated in Washington,
D.C.

**4/84 ....I spoke for the first time at my daughter, Jessica's,
seventh grade social studies class about my experi-
ences in Vietnam.**

**1/91 ....Cynthia, Jessica, and I visit the Vietnam Veterans
Memorial.**

**2/96 ....I meet Randy on the bus and soon thereafter wrote
out my first story.**

3/96-8/00..........I wrote this book.

Glossary

(Not all terms are used in the text)

A-4: Douglas "Skyhawk," a single-seat, light jet attack aircraft.

Agent Orange: One of several types of defoliating chemicals used by the U.S. military to deny the enemy vegetative cover for hiding. The chemicals were extremely powerful herbicides that also caused extensive neurological and genetic damage to humans and animals. Its greatest effects were on the Vietnamese.

a-gunner: An assistant gunner for a crew-served weapon such as a machine gun, mortar, artillery, or rocket launcher.

AIT: Advanced infantry training.

AK-47: Soviet Kalashnikov assault rifle supplied to the North Vietnamese Army and the Viet Cong, also called AKs.

ao dai: A traditional, semi-formal Vietnamese dress for women consisting of pants and a long blouse with slits on the sides.

APC: Armored personnel carrier including the M113 Armored Cavalry Assault Vehicle

arty: Refers to both the artillery pieces and the crews that fired them.

ARVN: Army of the Republic of Vietnam. Allied with the forces from the U.S., Australia, and South Korea.

azimuth: The horizontal angular distance from a fixed reference direction to a position. For the 81 mm mortar, it was the angle in degrees from the aiming stakes, which were set at due north and south, to the target direction.

B-52: Boeing "Stratofortress," an U.S. Air Force eight-engine, swept-wing, heavy jet bomber.

beans and motherfuckers: Combat ration delicacy composed of lima beans and chunks of ham.

beehive rounds: An explosive artillery shell which delivered thousands of small projectiles shaped like nails with fins, instead of shrapnel.

bends and motherfuckers: The squat-thrust exercise.

big boys: Artillery, "arty."

blow in place: Unexploded ordinance (duds) was blown up where it lay by timed explosives, typically C-4. This prevented the duds from injuring friendly troops and eliminated their use by the enemy for making mines.

boondocks or boonies: Away from the rear or more secure areas.

boot: A soldier just out of boot camp, inexperienced, untested.

Bouncing Betty: A homemade mine about the size of a soda can that was generally triggered by a trip wire. It sprang up to groin height before exploding.

brown bar: A lieutenant. Sometimes called a butter bar denoting the single brass bar of the rank. In the field, officers wore camouflage rank, which was often brown or black instead of brass.

bush: Boondocks.

busting caps: Firing a weapon; a reference probably derived from the paper percussion caps used in toy guns.

C4: A plastique explosive that was set off by an electrically-charged blasting cap. When lit, it would burn like Sterno.

C-rats: Combat rations.

capping: Shooting at the enemy.

Caribou: A small transport plane for moving men and materiel.

Charlie: Refers to the Viet Cong. Charlie is radio jargon for the letter "C," which stood for Cong.

cherry: Slang used to denote youth, inexperience, and virginity.

chu ho: "I surrender;" not a literal translation.

CO: Commanding Officer.

Cobra: A helicopter gunship, AH-1G.

cordite: A smokeless explosive powder that in its processed form resembles brown twine.

corpsman: Navy medics who served with the Marines.

deuce-and-a-half: A two-and-a-half-ton military truck.

diddy-bopping: Carelessly walking.

didi mau: Pidgin Vietnamese for escape or leave quickly.

D.I.: Drill Instructor.

dinks: Racist term for Vietnamese.

dinky dao: Pidgin Vietnamese for "crazy."

DMZ: Demilitarized Zone along the 17th Parallel that temporarily separated North Vietnam from South Vietnam. Established by the Geneva Accords of 1954.

doo-mommie: An English approximation of the Vietnamese words "du ma," meaning literally, fuck mother.

dopers: Those who used marijuana. Also known as "heads."

double veteran: Having sex with a woman and then killing her made one a double veteran.

EM club: Enlisted men's club.

F-4B: McDonnell "Phantom II," a twin-engine, two-seat, long-range jet interceptor and attack bomber.

fields of fire: A method of dividing land beyond a defensive perimeter. Each defender was assigned a wedge of land to cover with his weapon to insure no gaps existed.

finger charge: Explosive booby-trapping device which takes its name from its size and shape being approximately that of a man's finger.

Fire Operations Center: The bunker on a fire support base that protected people responsible for communications and calculating firing solutions for the mortars and artillery.

fleshette: A mine without great explosive power containing small pieces of shrapnel intended to wound and kill.

FNG: Acronym for "fucking new guy." Seniority in country was extremely important. Anyone fresh to Vietnam was considered less valuable than a "short-timer," one with only a short time remaining in his tour of duty. The thinking was that if you're going to die, you might as well do it early on and avoid the pain of war.

forward observer: The person responsible for spotting enemy targets and directing artillery to them.

frag: A fragmentation grenade. To attempt to kill with a fragmentation grenade or other weapon.

friendly fire: Rounds and shells accidentally aimed at ones own troops.

fugazi: Fucked up or screwed up.

gooks: Racist term for Vietnamese, passed down from the Korean War to Vietnam.

grenade pits: A small pit dug at the base of the entry ramp to an underground bunker. An enemy grenade would roll into the pit where most of its explosive force would be absorbed.

GR Point: Graves Registration Point; that place on a military base where the identification, embalming, and processing of dead soldiers takes place as part of the operations of the quartermaster.

grunt: Infantryman.

gung ho: Highly motivated (Chinese for "work together")

halizone: A tablet used to kill pathogens in drinking water.

H&I: Harassment and interdiction. Artillery bombardments used to deny the enemy terrain which they might find beneficial to their campaign. The targets for H&I were general rather than specific, confirmed military targets. H & I accounted for ninety percent of the artillery fired in Vietnam.

HE: High explosive rounds.

heads: Those who used marijuana. Also known as dopers.

hooch: Tents and shacks used to house military personnel in base camps; also used to refer to the thatch and bamboo homes of the rural Vietnamese.

hoochgirl: Young Vietnamese woman employed by American military as maid and laundress.

Huey (UH-1): All-purpose helicopter. Usually carried a pilot, co-pilot, one or two M-60 machine gunners, and up to eight troops with gear.

hump: March (verb and noun).

incoming: Enemy fire coming in. Also used as a general alarm to take cover.

in-country: Term to denote being in Vietnam.

jungle boots: Footwear that looks like a combination of combat boot and canvas sneaker used by the U.S. military in tropical climates, where leather rots because of the dampness. The canvas structure also speeds drying.

jungle utilities: Lightweight, tropical fatigues.

juicers: Alcohol drinkers as opposed to marijuana users (heads or dopers).

K-Bar: A military knife with an eight-inch blade.

KIA: Killed in action.

klick: Kilometer, 1,000 meters, 0.62 miles.

lifer: A career officer or long-term enlistee.

LP: Listening post.

LRPs: Members of Long Range Reconnaissance Patrols.

LZ: Landing zone. Usually a small clearing secured temporarily for the landing of resupply helicopters. LZs on base camps had large interlocking steel plates for a base.

M1: The standard U.S. infantryman's weapon in World War II. It fires a high-velocity .30 Cal. round.

M14: The standard U.S. infantryman's weapon after the Korean War. It fires the NATO standard high-velocity 7.62 mm round.

M16: The standard U.S. infantryman's weapon in Vietnam. A lightweight semi-automatic and automatic rifle manufactured by Colt Firearms that fires a high-velocity 5.56 mm round.

M60: A machine gun that fires a 7.62 mm round.

M79: A 40 mm grenade launcher.

mama san: Pidgin Vietnamese used by American servicemen for any older Vietnamese woman.

medevac: Evacuation of wounded via helicopter.

MIA: Missing in action.

mike-mike: Military jargon for millimeter (mm).

minigun: A gun with six rotating barrels based on the idea of Richard Gatling, the originator of the Gatling gun. It was capable of firing 6,000 rounds per minute.

Montagnard: Indigenous hill-dwelling people of Indochina.

MOS: Military occupational specialty. For 81 mm mortar crewmen, their MOS is 0341, "03" implies infantry, "41" for the 81.

MP: Military police.

number ten: Implies the worst possible thing, as opposed to number one, the best possible thing.

NVA: North Vietnamese regular army. Allied with the Viet Cong and China.

one-oh-five, one-oh-six, one-five-five, etc.: Artillery pieces: 105 mm, 106 mm, 155 mm.

P-38: Name given a small can opener that came with combat rations.

papa san: Pidgin Vietnamese used by U.S. servicemen for any older Vietnamese man.

pogey bait: Name for candy and sweets.

pogue: Derogatory term for military personnel employed in rear echelon support capacities.

point man: The first man in line as a squad or platoon of men walk along a trail or through the jungle.

Puller, Lewis B. (Chesty): A famous and highly-decorated Marine general who was the Commander of the 1st Marine Division.

pseudomonas: A genus of bacteria causing various suppurative infections in humans. Its presence gives pus a blue-green color.

PX: Post exchange. A military store.

rack: Bed or cot.

R & R: Rest and relaxation. Servicemen earned one week of R & R during a full tour of duty in Vietnam.

rear area: Relatively secure base areas.

rotation date: The last day of a tour of duty in Vietnam.

ROTC: Reserve Officer Training Corps.

rocket propelled grenades (RPG): A type of rocket used by the Viet Cong and NVA similar to the bazooka of World War II.

ROK: The Republic of Korea (South Korea) was one of the U.S. allies that sent troops to Vietnam.

salty: A seasoned soldier. Experienced. The opposite of a "cherry" or FNG.

sapper: Soldiers who try to infiltrate the perimeter defenses of a fortified position.

Sea Knight: Boeing Vertol CH-46, a twin-turbine, tandem rotor, medium transport helicopter.

Semper fidelis (often shortened to Semper fi): U.S. Marine Corps slogan meaning in Latin "always faithful."

Sgt. Rock: A combat-scarred World War II comic book character.

shaped charge: An explosive charge, the energy of which is focused in one direction.

short-timer: A soldier with less than two months remaining in his tour of duty. The less time remaining, the "shorter" he became. A saying was "I'm so short, I have to wear a raincoat in case the ants piss on me."

short-timer's stick: When a soldier had approximately two months remaining of his tour in Vietnam, he might take a long stick and notch it for each of his remaining days in-country. As each day passed, he would cut the stick off another notch until on his rotation day he was left with only a small stub.

six-by: A large flatbed truck usually with wooden slat sides enclosing the bed and sometimes a canvas top covering it, used for carrying men or anything else that would fit on it.

slick: slang for helicopter.

slopes: Racist term for Asians.

Spooky: A large propeller-driven aircraft (typically the AC-47) fitted with three miniguns in the side. Also used to refer to helicopter gunships equipped with miniguns. Known as Puff the Magic Dragon.

swagger stick: A short stick carried by some officers and Marine Corps Drill Instructors.

TC: Tactical commander.

Tet: Vietnamese for the lunar New Year.

thermite: A mixture of powdered aluminum and metal oxide, which produces great heat for use in welding and incendiary bombs.

TOC: Tactical operations center.

Top: A top sergeant.

tracer: A bullet chemically treated to leave a trail of smoke or fire to let the gunner see the direction of fire. The North Vietnamese Army and Viet Cong generally used green tracer rounds, Allied forces used primarily yellow and red.

tunnel rat: Someone who goes into an enemy tunnel.

unbloused: Pants not tucked into boot tops.

USO: United Service Organization. A private organization with the mission of providing entertainment and other services to U.S. military personnel.

Vietnam: Also spelled as "Viet Nam" and referred to as "Nam" or "the Nam." To be in Vietnam was to be "in-country."

ville: Short for village, indicating any location from a small town of several hundred inhabitants to a few thatched huts in a clearing.

VC, Viet Cong or, using radio call letters for the abbreviation, Victor Charlie: A contraction of the Vietnamese phrase meaning "Vietnamese Communist." Also, the National Liberation Front. The VC were people living in South Vietnam who were fighting in the south against the Republic of Vietnam's forces and its allies including the U.S.

We Do Care: Organized in 1969 and still lead today by Harriet Beekman, We Do Care is a volunteer social service group that sends packages of needed supplies, treats, and local newspapers to service personnel stationed over seas. In 1970, the group developed in Fairview Park, Ohio (a suburb of Cleveland) what they claim is the country's first Vietnam Veterans Memorial.

white phosphorus ("Willie Peter" using radio jargon): An artillery shell that produces an intense fire and large cloud of white smoke. Used for marking and adjusting for fire.

the World: The United States.

Bibliography

Baker, Mark. *Nam: The Vietnam War in the Words of the Men and Women Who Fought There*. New York: Berkley Books, 1981.

Barnet, Richard J. *Intervention and Revolution: America's Confrontation with Insurgent Movements Around the World* (revised and updated). New York: Meridian, 1968, 1972.

Bartlett, Tom, Gunnery Sergeant, USMC. "Dateline: Vietnam." *Leatherneck*, May 1969.

———"Operation Dewey Canyon." *Leatherneck*, February 1994.

———"War in the Fourth Year." *Leatherneck*, March 1994.

———"Nam Speak: A Forgotten Language?" *Leatherneck*, July 1994.

———"Turn Around and There You Are." *Leatherneck*, November 1994.

Bowman, John S. *The World Almanac of the Vietnam War*. New York: Pharos Books, 1985.

Boyer, Dwight. *Ghost Ships of the Great Lakes*. New York: Dodd, Mead & Company, 1968.

Bunting, Eve. *The Wall*. New York: Clarion Books, 1990.

Camp Pendleton—On the Way to Vietnam. Oceanside, California: Stewart Enterprises, (not dated).

Campbell, Joseph. *The Power of Myth with Bill Moyers*. Betty Sue Flowers, ed. New York: Doubleday, 1988.

Capps, Walter, ed. *The Vietnam Reader*. New York: Routledge, 1990.

Caputo, Phillip. *A Rumor of War*. New York: Ballantine Books, 1977.

Cohen, Steven, ed. *Vietnam: Anthology and Guide to a Television History*. New York: Alfred A. Knopf, 1983.

Davis, Gordon M., First Lieutenant USMC. "Dewey Canyon: All Weather Classic." *Marine Corps Gazette*, July 1969.

Findlay, R.F., Jr., Major USMC. "Behind the Hedgerow." *Marine Corps Gazette*, April 1969.

Fitzgerald, Frances. *Fire in the Lake: The Vietnamese and the Americans in Vietnam*. New York: Random House, 1973.

Generous, Kevin M. *Vietnam: The Secret War*. New York: Gallery Books, 1985.

Green, Wallace M. III, Major USMC. "Countermeasures Against Mines and Boobytraps." *Marine Corps Gazette*, December 1969.

Greenberg, Martin H., and Augustus Richard Norton, ed. *Touring Nam*. New York: William Morrow, 1985.

Grossman, Dave, Lieutenant Colonel. *On Killing: The Psychological Cost of Learning to Kill in War and Society*. Boston: Little, Brown and Company, 1995, 1996.

Hanh, Thich Nhat. *Peace is Every Step: The Path of Mindfulness in Daily Life*. New York: Bantam Books, 1991.

Heyslip, Le Ly. *When Heaven and Earth Changed Places: A Vietnamese Woman's Journey from War to Peace*. New York: Doubleday, 1989.

Herr, Michael. *Dispatches*. New York: Avon Book, 1978.

Herring, George C. *America's Longest War*. New York: Alfred A. Knopf, 1979.

History and Museums Division Headquarters, USMC. *Marines in Vietnam, 1954-1973, An Anthology and Annotated Bibliography*. Washington, D.C.: 1974.

Jaunnal, Jack W., Sergeant Major USMC (Ret.). "One Large Success in a Lost War." *Marine Corps Gazette*, November 1978.

Karnow, Stanley. *Vietnam: A History*. New York: The Viking Press, 1983.

Kerry, John and Vietnam Veterans Against the War. *The New Soldier*. New York: Collier Books, 1971.

Kriegel, Richard C., Lieutenant Colonel USMC. "Vietnamese Attitudes and Behavior." *Marine Corps Gazette*, April 1969.

LaFeber, Walter. *America, Russia, and the Cold War 1945—1980* (4th Edition). New York: John Wiley & Sons, 1967, 1972, 1976, 1980.

Lawliss, Chuck. *The Marine Book: A Portrait of America's Military Elite.* New York: Thames and Hudson, 1988.

Lopes, Sal. *The Wall.* New York: Collins Publishers, 1987.

MacPherson, Myra. *Long Time Passing.* Chicago: Signet, 1984.

Mason, J.D. "V.C. Trail." *Marine Corps Gazette*, April 1969.

Meyers, Bruce F., Colonel USMC. "Jungle Canopy Operations." *Marine Corps Gazette*, July 1969.

Michener, James A. *Kent State: What Happened and Why.* New York: Random House, 1971.

Moskin, J. Robert. *The Marine Corps Story.* New York: McGraw-Hill Book Company, 1987

Nicoli, Robert V., Major USMC. "Fire Support Base Development." *Marine Corps Gazette*, September 1969.

O'Brien, Tim. *Going After Cacciato.* New York: Dell Publishing Co., 1975.

———*The Things They Carried.* New York: Penguin Books, 1990.

O'Neal, Don, Staff Sergeant USMC. "Allied Troops, 'Dozers Clear Dodge City." *Sea Tiger* published by the III Marine Amphibious Force, Vietnam, 11 July 1969.

Page, Tim, and John Pimlott, ed. *Nam, the Vietnam Experience 1965-75.* London: Barnes and Noble Books, 1995.

Richardson, Herb, Gunnery Sergeant USMC. "Meade River." *Leatherneck*, April 1969.

Sayres, Sohnya, Anders Stephanson, Stanley Aronowitz, Fredrick Jameson, ed. *The 60s Without Apology*. Minneapolis: University of Minnesota Press, 1984.

Sheehan, Neil. *A Bright Shining Lie*. New York: Vintage Books, 1988.

Sien-chong, Niu. "Mao's Mobile Warfare." *Marine Corps Gazette*, April 1969.

Simmons, Edward H., Brigadier General USMC (Ret.). *Marine Corps Operations in Vietnam, 1969-1972*. Reprinted from Naval Review, U.S. Naval Institute, 1973.

Simmons, Edward H., Brigadier General USMC. *The Illustrated History of Marines, the Vietnam War*. Washington, D.C.: United States Marine Corps, 1987.

Smolan, Rick and Jennifer Erwitt. *Passage to Vietnam*. Hong Kong: Against All Odds Productions, 1994.

Summers, Harry G. Jr., Colonel of Infantry. *Vietnam War Almanac*. New York: Facts on File Publications, 1985.

Welsh, Douglas. *The Vietnam War*. London: Bison Books Ltd, 1982.

Ye, Ting-Xing. *A Leaf in the Bitter Wind: A Memoir*. Saint Paul, Minnesota: Hungry Mind Press, 1997.

About the Author

J. Michael Orange served in the United States Marine Corps from 1968 to 1970 including a twelve month tour of duty from March 1969 to March 1970 in Vietnam. As the squad leader for an 81 mm mortar platoon, he was awarded a meritorious combat promotion to corporal during Operation Durham Peak in the Que Son Mountains. Later he became Section Leader of the Second Section.

After his discharge, Mr. Orange witnessed the events precedent to the shootings at Kent State University and actively participated in the peace movement until the War's end in 1975. He participated in the famed 1971 march on Washington when for the first time in this country's history, veterans protested against the war they fought and threw their medals back over the Capital fence.

Since 1984, Mr. Orange has studied the War including completing history classes at Metropolitan State University. Annually, he volunteers as a guest lecturer for high school history and social studies classes speaking on the topic of the Vietnam War and peace movement with a focus on his own experiences and personal research.

Currently, Mr. Orange is a senior planner with nearly twenty-five years of experience with the Minneapolis Planning Department. After completing four years at Borromeo High School Seminary in Cleveland, Ohio, Mr. Orange earned his B. A. degree from Kent State University in Kent, Ohio and his M. A. in Urban and Regional Studies from Mankato State University in Mankato, Minnesota.

Michael and his wife, Cynthia Orange, live in St. Paul, Minnesota. Their daughter, Jessica, is currently a graduate student at Mills College in Oakland, California.

Printed in the United States
28717LVS00004B/64-120

9 780595 160037